GLASGOW

A Book Trust Scotland Literary Guide to authors and books associated with the city

by Moira Burgess
with a foreword by Alan Spence

reading
GLASGOW

A Book Trust Scotland Literary Guide
to books and writers associated with the city
by Moira Burgess
with a foreword by Alan Spence

© Book Trust Scotland 1996

Published by Book Trust Scotland
Scottish Book Centre
137 Dundee Street
Edinburgh EH11 1BG

Edited by Liffy Grant
Design by Ann Ross Paterson
Printed by Macdonald Lindsay Pindar

This is one of a series of Literary Guides to Scotland,
published by Book Trust Scotland.
For details of other Book Trust Publications: send a sae to Book Trust Scotland,
Scottish Book Centre, 137 Dundee Street, Edinburgh EH11 1BG

Book Trust Scotland gratefully acknowledges the help and expertise of
Ann Escott of the Glasgow Room at the Mitchell Library;
Elizabeth Watson of the Special Collections Department of the
University of Glasgow and Winnie Tyrrell of the Photolibrary,
Glasgow Museums.

We are also indebted to the following authors for their invaluable contributions
to the guide; Robert Crawford, Margaret Thomson Davis, Pat Gerber,
Cliff Hanley, David Kinloch, Liz Lochhead, Edwin Morgan, Frank Rodgers,
Margaret Ryan, Alan Spence and Derick Thomson.

Every effort has been made to trace copyright ownership and
we would be grateful to learn of any unwitting infringement.

Book Trust Scotland is very grateful for the financial assistance given by the
Scottish Arts Council, The Caram Charitable Trust, John Smith & Son Ltd,
Booksellers, Glasgow and Mitchells Roberton, Solicitors, Glasgow in the
publication of this guide.

Contents

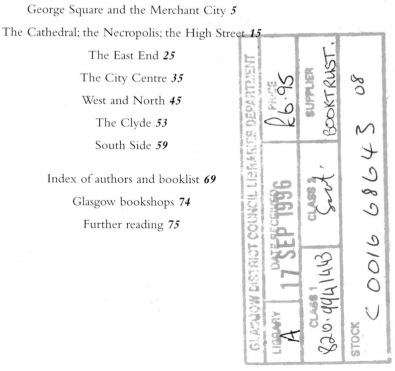

The cover of this book shows a detail from *MARCH - Spirit of the Community* a banner designed by Malcolm Lochhead and Joseph Davie from *Keeping Glasgow in Stitches* a joint project organised by NeedleWorks Ltd and Glasgow Museums in 1990. It shows the symbols which appear on Glasgow's Coat of Arms - the tree, the bird, the book, the bell and the fish. Each relates to St Mungo, Glasgow's patron saint and appear in the rhyme which is familiar to generations of Glasgow school children:

> Here's the Tree that never grew,
> Here's the Bird that never flew;
> Here's the Bell that never rang,
> Here's the Fish that never swam.

The tree was once the bough which, when frozen, Mungo blew into flame and with which he lit St Serf's Monastery lamps. The bird is St Serf's robin restored to life by Mungo in his youth. The fish and the ring refer to the story of Queen Langueth. She sought Mungo's help after a ring, given to her by her husband King Rhydderch, was lost in the Clyde. It was recovered in the mouth of a salmon. The bell was brought by Mungo from Rome. The mound on which he is standing is the ground miraculously raised by Mungo while addressing the people on his return from Rome. This gave rise to the motto 'Let Glasgow Flourish by the Preaching of the Word.' It is commonly thought that the book is the Bible.

When these bearings were formally registered as the City's Coat of Arms in 1866, the only important change was the motto which was shortened to 'Let Glasgow Flourish'.

Foreword

Glasgow's full of poets, wrote Alan Jackson back in the 1960s. *They're three foot high and eat sherbet dabs.* A wry Edinburgh take, perhaps, on that *other* city's notion of itself, written, ironically, at a time when a whole generation of writers was indeed beginning to emerge.

Among them was Alasdair Gray who was to write a memorable passage in *Lanark*, in which Duncan Thaw complains that no-one *imagines* living in Glasgow, not in the same way as in Florence, Paris, London, New York. He continues, *Imaginatively Glasgow exists as a music-hall song and a few bad novels. That's all we've given to the world outside. It's all we've given to ourselves.*

Well, much of that has changed, and continues to change. Love the place or hate it (or both!), the city has seen what Moira Burgess describes here as a "perfect explosion of talent". For a whole generation of writers (and artists, musicians, film-makers) the city's *imaginative existence* is now a given, a starting-point. How and why this has come about, she rightly argues, are matters for a literary history of the city. (Now *there's* a task!) And what a book might be made of Glasgow's hidden, lost or suppressed writing - the kind of job done so well by Tom Leonard in *Radical Renfrew*.

What Moira Burgess has done here is take another approach. For her too, Glasgow's imaginative existence, its literature, is given. What she offers is a guidebook to that literature, not arranged chronologically, but geographically, district by district. It's a daunder round the city, a look at its writers, in the company of an entertaining and thoroughly well-versed guide - the city as an open book.

It is full of wonderful little anecdotes, glimpses which show the city and its writers in a fresh light. I'll never again pass the Sarry Heid - the Saracen's Head pub - on my way to the Barrows or Parkhead, without picturing Adam Smith being thrown out for swearing at Dr. Johnson, calling him "a son of a bitch!".

Or imagine De Quincey in his lodgings, wasted on laudunum, complaining to his landlady and insisting she "cut the mutton in a diagonal rather than longitudinal form".

There are sites too associated with Burns - a tomb stone in the Old Vennel in Pollokshaws marks the grave of his daughter by Anna Park. And we are reminded that the "Clarinda" of *Ae Fond Kiss* was from Glasgow.

And there are haunting images - the "pedlar poet" James Macfarlan, described by a contemporary as a "ragged, unkempt, mean-looking tramp", yet one in whom "the divine fire burned with unquenchable flame". (Today he'd be publishing his poems in *The Big Issue*.)

It's the juxtaposition of these disparate images as we move through the book, through the city and its past, that make the place come to life. Whatever Glasgow you're looking for - dear green place or no mean city, Unthank or Clydegrad, patter-merchant-city of culture, or city of the stare, this book can only add to its "imaginative existence".

Alan Spence June 1996

Moira Burgess was born in Campbeltown but
has lived in Glasgow for many years, working
first as a librarian and later as a freelance writer
while bringing up her family. A novelist and
short story writer, she is also an authority on
Glasgow fiction and her bibliography *The
Glasgow Novel* (2nd edition 1986) is regarded as a
standard work in its field. With Hamish Whyte
she has edited two anthologies of Glasgow short
stories, *Streets of Stone* (1985) and *Streets of Gold*
(1989). She compiled *Glasgow Books and
Writers of the Twentieth Century* for
Book Trust Scotland in 1990.

She is interested in Glasgow history and
architecture and writes in her essay "The
Novelists' Map of Glasgow" (in *A Glasgow
Collection*, edited by McCarra and Whyte 1990)
about her fondness of "going about Glasgow on
foot, or on top of a bus". She much enjoyed using
the same approach in compiling *reading Glasgow*.

Introduction

It would be good if we could take, like scientists, a core sample of the literary history of Glasgow. What has happened over the centuries, and why? There have been lean years (and decades), but there have been spells when the place seemed crammed with writers.

Here are the nineteenth-century "poetry shops" like the Poet's Box, and the ballad criers like Hawkie and Jamie Blue who declaimed poetry in the streets. Here, around the same time, is the Whistle-Binkie group, sublimely unaware that in another hundred years their work would be execrated as everything that Scottish poetry ought not to be. Here's the slightly later group of writers encouraged and published by James Hedderwick, no great writer himself but what we would now call an excellent facilitator. Here are the proletarian novelists of the 1920s and 1930s, trying with varying degrees of success to tackle the industrial city, and the radical Clyde Group of the forties. Here's a perfect explosion of talent in the 1960s and 1970s, whose vibrations have not yet died away; what on earth caused that? Here's a similar outburst of young dramatists - Iain Heggie, Chris Hannan, Marcella Evaristi and others - kick-starting an area of Glasgow writing which had until then been rather underplayed. Here's the present day, with writers' groups and workshops all over the city, not confined to the traditional haunts of the literati. Are they the voice of the people? Are they influenced by earlier literary history, or responding to quite other stimuli?

So far, critics might say, so parochial; but here and there we can see a blip in the reading, where Glasgow seems to become, for good or ill, part of a wider world. Adam Smith is chucked out of the pub after a wordy row with Dr. Johnson. William Miller writes "Wee Willie Winkie", part of everyone's childhood. J.J.Bell writes *Wee Macgreegor,* which becomes a household name here and overseas. In case all these wee weans are making things too cosy, here's Alexander McArthur with *No Mean City*, providing the world with a perception of Glasgow which still hasn't quite gone away. Hugh MacDiarmid absolutely hates Glasgow (as do Edwin Muir and Lewis Grassic Gibbon). But here's Alasdair Gray with *Lanark*, turning Glasgow fiction inside-out, and there's Edwin Morgan bringing an international and extraterrestrial dimension to Glasgow writing, certainly to international acclaim, though reports from other galaxies have yet to be received. (Incidentally, Morgan's poem "Rider" is a surrealistic look at Glasgow poetry over the years.)

Since a book of this size cannot possibly provide such a literary history, we have taken an alternative approach here, that of the guidebook, looking at the city where these writers lived and wrote. Generally, in each section, we have considered first what traces of them remain, and then what traces of the city can be found in their work. Again for reasons of space, coverage can only be sketchy. However, through listings of local authors (whether mentioned in the text or not) and suggestions for further reading, we hope that interested readers can start from here to explore the fascinating and relatively uncharted world of Glasgow literature.

George Square and the Merchant City

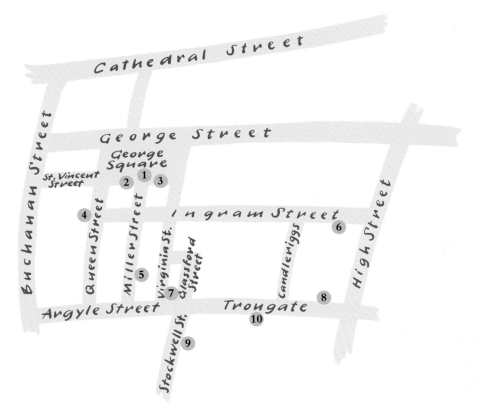

1. Walter Scott
2. Robert Burns
3. Thomas Campbell
4. Alexander Smith
5. Stirling's Library
6. Ramshorn Church
7. (Site of) the Black Bull Inn
8. (Site of) James Brash & William Reid's Trongate Bookshop
9. Scotia Bar
10. William Black

George Square, the civic centre of Glasgow, is not necessarily the city's literary centre, but there is no missing the literary monument at its heart. The eight-foot-high column supporting a statue of Sir Walter Scott, erected in 1837, was the first memorial to this giant of Scottish literature. The inscription reads simply WALTER SCOTT, as if that, five years after his death, was all that needed to be said. Many Glasgow people will tell you that the statue shows Scott's plaid on the wrong shoulder, and that the sculptor killed himself in shame on discovering the mistake. The story is a

George Square, dome of the City Chambers in the foreground DONALD CLEMENTS

Sir Walter Scott by Sir Henry Raeburn SCOTTISH NATIONAL PORTRAIT GALLERY

myth, however since Scott was a Borderer, and Border shepherds - unlike Highlanders - wore the plaid on the right shoulder, not the left.

Scott's great popularity during his lifetime and his lasting reputation are probably good enough reasons for his statue's pride of place, though Glasgow, of course, was neither his birthplace nor his home. He did visit the city from time to time, and evidently observed some of its people well. The character of the Glasgow merchant Bailie Nicol Jarvie, in *Rob Roy*, springs to life on the page. We shall meet the Bailie later in this tour, in the Saltmarket and the old streets around Glasgow Cathedral which Scott used as the setting for part of *Rob Roy*.

Similarly, it is perhaps national fame, rather than strictly local connections, which justifies the statue of Robert Burns set up in George Square in 1877. Burns is shown as a countryman in homespun clothes, carrying a Kilmarnock bonnet in his right hand. In his left hand he should be holding a daisy, as he composes his lines to the "wee, modest, crimson-tipped flow'r", but unfortunately the flower is detachable and all too often becomes detached. The bronze reliefs on the base of the statue are worth looking at. On the east there is a lively scene from "Tam o'Shanter", on the west a quiet family group "The Cottar's Saturday Night". On the north side Burns sits in his cottage - "ben i' the spence", that is, through in the inner room - looking into the fire while a Muse crowns him with holly (not laurel, because she is a Scottish Muse). This is an illustration of his poem "The Vision", in which Burns describes his Muse with verve and disrespect:

> Down flow'd her robe, a tartan sheen,
> Till half a leg was scrimply seen;
> And such a leg!. . .

The bonnie Muse and the domestic details - the kettle on the range, dog by the chair - make a pleasant picture in the busy Square.

Like Scott, Burns visited Glasgow now and then, staying in the Black Bull Inn, whose site in Argyle Street we shall note later in this tour. Another Glasgow myth assures us that he first tried to get his poems printed by the local bookseller,

Robert Burns by Alexander Nasmyth SCOTTISH NATIONAL PORTRAIT GALLERY

publisher and poet William Reid, but no evidence has been found to support this. However, his much-admired "Clarinda" - Mrs Nancy Maclehose, whom he met in Edinburgh and for whom he wrote "Ae Fond Kiss" - was a Glasgow girl, daughter of the surgeon Andrew Craig, and her husband was a Glasgow lawyer. We shall find an even more interesting Burns connection when we visit the South Side.

"Clarinda" Nancy Maclehose from James Kilpatrick's *Literary Landmarks of Glasgow* GLASGOW CITY LIBRARIES

"I'll ne'er blame my partial fancy
Naething could resist my Nancy
But to see her, was to love her;
Love but her, and love for ever
Ae fond kiss, and then we sever;
Ae farewell, and then for ever!"

from *Ae Fond Kiss* written by Robert Burns

The third literary monument in George Square commemorates Thomas Campbell, who can certainly be claimed as a Glasgow poet. He was born near High Street, not very far from the Square where he has stood beside Burns since 1871, in Regency dress, pensively holding a quill pen and a sheaf of manuscript. Much less famous now than Scott or Burns, Thomas Campbell nevertheless had his hour of fame, when his martial poems "Hohenlinden" and "Ye mariners of England", and the richly romantic "Lord Ullin's Daughter", were known to every schoolchild. He lived for much of his life in London and is buried in Westminster Abbey, but returned to Glasgow in 1826 when he was elected Lord Rector of Glasgow University, the scene of his brilliant early career.

Thomas Campbell by Sir Thomas Lawrence
SCOTTISH NATIONAL PORTRAIT GALLERY

Attending a dinner given by Thomas Campbell, Professor John Wilson (Christopher North) was much struck by the attractive maid Margaret; "I [Campbell] ran to get refreshments for them and fair Margaret brought them in. The professor looked at her with so much admiration that I told him in Latin to contain his raptures, and he did so; but rose and walked round the room like a lion pacing his cage. . . Before parting he said 'Could not you just ring and get me a sight of that vision of beauty again?' 'No, no,' I told him 'get you gone, you Moral Philosopher loon, and give my best respects to your wife and daughter!' "

from *The Life and Letters of Thomas Campbell*

George Square is on the edge of the Merchant City, where the foundations of Glasgow's prosperity were laid in the eighteenth and early nineteenth centuries through the tobacco and textile trades. Here and there, interestingly, the mercantile and literary worlds intersect. At 77 Queen Street a plaque high up on the right of the entrance to South Exchange Court marks where one of Glasgow's best poets spent some of his non-poetical hours.

ALEXANDER SMITH

1827-1867

POET AND ESSAYIST

WORKED IN THIS BUILDING AS A

MUSLIN PATTERN-DESIGNER

FROM 1846 UNTIL 1853

"A SACREDNESS OF LOVE AND DEATH

DWELLS IN THY NOISE AND SMOKY BREATH"

The quoted lines are from Smith's poem "Glasgow", one of the earliest to deal with the industrial city.

Alexander Smith portrait from *City Poems* GLASGOW CITY LIBRARIES

Smith was extravagantly praised for his early work "A Life Drama". He sold the copyright for £100, and accepted the post offered to him of Secretary to Edinburgh University. The salary was small and Smith, who married about this time, had to write continuously, as well as working a full day at the University, to support his wife and family. An almost inevitable backlash to his early fame meant that his later work tended to be undervalued in his lifetime. More recently his *City Poems* (including "Glasgow") and the prose work *A Summer in Skye*, which also contains vivid descriptions of Glasgow, have begun to receive the recognition they deserve.

East of Queen Street we are in the Merchant City proper. In Miller Street we should acknowledge - as many Glasgow writers have done - the city's excellent library service, which may be said to have begun here. Walter Stirling, a wealthy merchant and Town Councillor, died in 1791 and bequeathed his house in Miller Street and his collection of books to establish a library to which the public would have free access, the first of its kind in Scotland. Stirling's Library began operations elsewhere in the city, but since 1844 it has been in or near Miller Street. First it moved to the site of Stirling's mansion (no.48-56 Miller Street, which replaced the old house in 1863, is still there), then across to no.21, which the Mitchell Library had just vacated (we shall catch up with the Mitchell later), then, in 1954, to the splendid surroundings of the Royal Exchange Building, not far away. Since 1994 Stirling's Library has been back in Miller Street, at no.62, almost next door to the site of its founder's house.

Along Ingram Street is Ramshorn Church, now a drama centre, but still retaining its

An interior shot of Stirling's Library when it was in Royal Exchange Square. The building is now the site of Glasgow's recently opened Gallery of Modern Art and Stirling's Library is nearby in Miller Street. DONALD CLEMENTS

eighteenth-century graveyard, older than the present church. William Glen, a Glasgow poet who wrote the Jacobite song "Wae's me for Prince Charlie", is buried here. So is Pierre Emile L'Angelier (though his name does not appear on the tombstone), whose mysterious death has given rise to novels, poems and plays for over a hundred years. We shall meet Madeleine Smith, tried in 1857 for his murder, later on.

The passer-by might easily miss another Ramshorn burial-place. On the Ingram Street pavement, outside the railings of the present graveyard, appear the initials RF AF and a cross. This dates from the nineteenth-century widening of Ingram Street, which took in part of the graveyard, and marks the grave of the brothers Robert and Andrew Foulis, eighteenth-century printers in Glasgow.

In 1741 the Foulis brothers, still in their twenties, set up as booksellers in

Interior of the Academy of the Fine Arts in the University of Glasgow
Above: Caricature portrait of *Andrew Foulis* BOTH IMAGES EDINBURGH CITY LIBRARIES

the University of Glasgow, which was then in the High Street. A year later Robert began his own printing business. The brothers were appointed as university printers, and their press gained a high, and lasting, reputation for its immaculate production and fine typography. (Some examples can still be readily seen in Glasgow, as we shall find.) In 1754, Robert set up the Foulis Academy of Fine Arts, but it survived for only some twenty years, consuming in the process most of the profits of the printing house.

The southern edge of the Merchant City is marked by Trongate and its continuation in Argyle Street. At the corner of Argyle Street and Virginia Street, on what is now a Marks & Spencer store, a plaque commemorates one of Glasgow's old inns (founded in 1758) and its literary connection.

ROBERT BURNS
LODGED HERE WHEN THIS
BUILDING WAS THE
BLACK BULL INN
➥

HE VISITED GLASGOW
JUNE 1787
➥

FEBRUARY AND MARCH 1788

Only a few years later James Brash and William Reid were publishing poems in "penny numbers" from their bookseller's shop in Trongate, which became a favourite meeting-place of Glasgow literati. A similar grouping formed about the middle of the nineteenth century, around the publisher David Robertson who originated the series of verse anthologies entitled Whistle-Binkie. The collections were immensely popular at the time, though in more recent years their combination of humour, sentimentality and satire has fallen out of favour. Glasgow poets such as William Motherwell and Alexander Rodger - whom we shall meet later - contributed to Whistle-Binkie, and "Wee Willie Winkie", the immortal nursery poem by William Miller, first appeared there in 1841.

This area of Glasgow seems to favour literary howffs. The Scotia Bar in Stockwell Street is a centre for writers, singers and musicians - its first Writers' Prize, awarded in 1990, resulted in the anthology *A Spiel Amang Us* - and poetry readings are held regularly in the nearby Clutha Vaults.

Trongate was the birthplace of William Black the novelist, whose works were great favourites with the Victorian reading public. Black began in local journalism, but went to London at the age of twenty-one to seek his fortune, with a group of young West of Scotland writers which included David Gray, Robert Buchanan and Charles Gibbon. Buchanan and Gibbon published essays, novels and plays which are little remembered now. Black, however, had an overnight success in 1871 with his fourth novel, *A Daughter of Heth*. Much of his work is set in the romantic West Highlands, with side-excursions to Glasgow; Black spent every spring and autumn in the Highlands, often taking notes for that year's book, and there is a monument to him, suitably, on Duart Point in Mull.

One eighteenth-century house, no.42, remains in Miller Street, but there are enough slightly later houses and imposing warehouses to make us wonder why only a few Glasgow writers have

been inspired by the buzzing life which these streets knew. Sarah Tytler, a prolific and popular Victorian novelist from Fife, was so inspired, and her novel *St Mungo's City* is a lively picture of the Glasgow of the textile trade. More recently, in *Wax Fruit*, Guy McCrone places one of his central characters, Arthur Moorhouse, in a warehouse in Candleriggs. (A country boy, he sensibly deals in "the produce of the farmlands: and people must eat, even in bad times".)

But it is Frederick Niven in his novels *Justice of the Peace* and *The Staff at Simson's* who most fully celebrates the Merchant City. Niven, on leaving school, spent some time "learning the business" in a textile warehouse, though never with great zeal.

> I began with winceys and it was Charlie Maclean, head of the wincey department, who informed me, gazing at me solemnly one day, "Freddy, the plain fact is that ye dinna gie a spittle for your work."

He soon moved on to a more congenial occupation in the Mitchell Library, later to journalism, and later still moved permanently to Canada for health reasons; but he had observed and remembered what he needed. *Justice of the Peace* links the stories of Ebenezer Moir "in his Glassford Street warehouse" and his son Martin, who wants to be an artist, as Niven also did for a time. *The Staff at Simson's* - Simson's textile warehouse in Cochrane Street - follows, in near-documentary fashion, the lives of its workers, from boss to office-boy, over some twenty years. These lively, readable, almost forgotten books bring the real Merchant City to life.

Glasgow Folk

Yes, yes, I know it has become a cliché to say Glasgow people are friendly but the fact remains that it is true.

Beginner writers say to me - "I don't know how you think up all the characters for your novels."

And I tell them that I don't need to. Glasgow is teeming with characters. I don't even need to go looking for them. I was wandering along one day, dreaming about one of my stories and I nearly went under a bus. A woman saved me by jerking me back just in the nick of time with the words - "You nearly got your coat pressed there, hen!"

Talking of buses, I would ask the stranger to forgive the occasional eccentricity of our Transport bosses, for instance, the notice that they have adorning all their vehicles at the moment. It says "Please do not wear roller skates in the bus." Never, in all the years of my travels have I seen one Glaswegian careering down the aisles in roller skates. (Mind you, I wouldn't be a bit surprised if I did!)

If I'm not travelling around in Public Transport, I'm on foot and I remember one time I'd stopped a woman to ask the way to some street or other. I write novels about Glasgow but I still can never remember where any place is.

This woman began to explain to me but was quickly joined by other interested Glaswegians who apparently felt they had a better way of explaining the directions. Soon there was a little knot of people around me, all intent on solving my problem. One gentleman even offered to escort me to my destination. This kind offer I declined because I suspected he had been enjoying a "wee refreshment" prior to joining the group and was in danger of becoming too friendly.

Talking of being friendly, I was sitting in a crowded bus and a Glasgow woman struggled breathlessly on, weighed down with a heavy shopping bag clutched in each hand. She looked along the bus as if she intimately knew every soul there, and confided - "This has been me since first thing this mornin'."

Another time an old woman sat down beside me and immediately said - "This is ma birthday the day." I congratulated her and she proceeded to tell me about how her daughter had taken her out to a pub for a "wee refreshment" to celebrate. "An' ah jist thought while ah wis there," she confided, "that if ony of ma neighbours saw me they'd look doon their noses at me fur bein' in a pub. But ah jist thought - what harm was ah doin' onybuddy, and so ah made up a poem aboot it and it goes somethin' like this . . ." And she launched into a poem in the defence of strong drink.

As I sat there listening and trying to contain my hilarity, I thought to myself - where else in the whole world could this happen, except on a Glasgow bus?

Glasgow folk, women in particular, I've always found, are very resourceful, and seldom stuck for words. I remember having a fascinating conservation with one woman. I think it was at a bus stop. As you'll have gathered, Public Transport plays an important in my life. I often get the plot of a whole novel while waiting for a bus. Anyway, this woman was chatting away, and at one point she was fuming about this dreadful husband and concluded by saying. "Ah jist huv nothin' to dae wi' him." I was a bit puzzled at this. "But you said you had seven children," I reminded her. She was non-plussed, but only for a moment. "Aye, but ye see," she said, "ah'm an awfi heavy sleeper."

She reminded of the big Buddha of a woman who used to live upstairs from my mother in our Glasgow tenement. This woman used to sit at her window watching the world pass by in the street below and make comments on it. I remember an old man shuffling past and she said - "Look at that lazy old sod. He's never done a day's work since he retired."

A fellow scribe, William McIlvanney, once said that Glasgow wasn't a city, it was a twenty-four hour cabaret. I think he might be right. One thing is certain, Glaswegians are God's gift to the novelist.

But if you are a non-Glaswegian, if you are a stranger who has just arrived in the city, or a traveller only passing through, a hundred thousand friendly welcomes.

Margaret Thomson Davis 1995

Margaret Thomson Davis' first novel *The Breadmakers* was published in 1972 and is still selling over twenty years later. With over 200 published short stories and 16 novels to her credit, she is also much in demand as a tutor and speaker. Her books, many of which are set in Glasgow, include *The Prince and the Tobacco Lords* (1976), *Roots of Bondage* (1977) and *Scorpion in the Fire* (1977) which were published as *The Tobacco Lords Trilogy* in 1994. *Kiss Me No More*, published in 1995, is the second of a planned trilogy which began with *Hold Me Forever* (1994).

The Cathedral, the Necropolis and the High Street

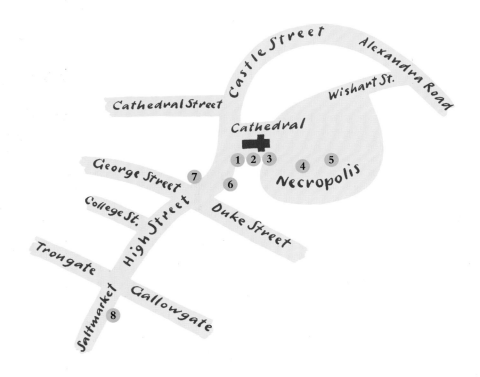

1. Zachary Boyd
2. Henry Glassford Bell
3. James Hedderwick
4. William Miller
5. William Motherwell
6. (Original site of) University
7. Thomas Campbell
8. Tobias Smollett

Glasgow began with the Cathedral, and the Cathedral has a link with the first book printed in Glasgow, Zachary Boyd's *Catechisms* of 1639. Zachary Boyd was minister of the Barony Church, which in his time had its premises in the crypt of the Cathedral. At different times he was Dean of Faculty, Rector and Vice-Chancellor of Glasgow University, and his manuscripts are preserved in the University Library. As well as being a preacher (he preached a vigorous sermon in 1650 against Oliver Cromwell, not at all deterred by Cromwell's presence in the congregation), he was known as a poet, particularly for *Zion's Flowers*, a rendering of Bible episodes into verse. It was

Necropolis, statue of John Knox in the foreground DONALD CLEMENTS

15

Zacharias Boyd author of *Catechisms*
the first book printed in Glasgow

known as Zachary Boyd's Bible. Bailie Nicol Jarvie in *Rob Roy* approves of it:

". . . the worthy Mr. Zachary Boyd's translation o' the Scriptures - better poetry need nane to be, as he had been tell'd by them that kend, or sud hae kend, about sic things."

from *Rob Roy* by Walter Scott

The Cathedral has always featured on the itinerary of visitors to Glasgow, who were not always appreciative of its beauties. Robert Southey, then poet laureate, paid it a visit in 1819, and remarked that "the seats are so closely packed that any who would remain there during the time of service in warm weather must have an invincible nose." Harriet Beecher Stowe, author of *Uncle Tom's Cabin*, was, she admitted, overtired when she saw it in 1853: "I could hardly walk through the building. . . Nothing is so utterly hazardous to a person's strength as looking at cathedrals." There are more enthusiastic descriptions, as we shall find.

Glasgow Cathedral

"On attaining the summit of the hill, we turned to the left, and a large pair of folding doors admitted us, amongst others, into the open and extensive burying-place which surrounds the Minster, or Cathedral Church of Glasgow. The pile is of a gloomy and massive, rather than of an elegant, style of Gothic architecture; but its peculiar character is so strongly preserved, and so well suited with the accompaniments that surround it, that the impression of the first view was awful and solemn in the extreme. I was indeed so much struck, that I resisted for a few minutes all Andrew's efforts to drag me into the interior of the building, so deeply was I engaged in surveying its outward character."

from *Rob Roy* by Walter Scott

Henry Glassford Bell
NATIONAL GALLERIES OF SCOTLAND

Amongst the many tombs and memorials in the Cathedral there are two of literary interest. A brass plate in the floor at the east end of the nave marks the grave of Henry Glassford Bell, a lawyer and a prolific writer of verse and prose. Not much of his work is now remembered, but Victorians knew and loved his poem "Mary Queen of Scots", which, in dramatic stanzas, relates the tragic queen's life step by step – "The scene is changed" – until her execution, with her pet dog sheltering under her skirt. James Hedderwick's memorial in the north aisle of the nave is worth noting. Hedderwick, a minor poet, is important as an editor. He founded the *Glasgow Citizen* as a weekly paper in 1842, and *Hedderwick's Miscellany* in 1862. In 1864, he launched the *Evening Citizen* on its long career, which lasted until 1974. The roll-call of Glasgow writers who had their first publication in Hedderwick's papers - Alexander Smith, Hugh Macdonald, David Wingate, James Macfarlan, William Black - assures him a place in Glasgow literary history. The bronze portrait medallion on his memorial shows a fine, strong, thoughtful old face.

James Hedderwick from *Backward Glances* by James Hedderwick
GLASGOW CITY LIBRARIES

Behind the Cathedral is Glasgow's most famous graveyard, the Necropolis, crowned by its statue of the reformer John Knox (who might be regarded as an author too, on the grounds of his writings against the "monstrous regiment of women"). Unfortunately, some of the monuments of literary interest here have been damaged by either weather or vandalism.

The monument to William Miller (who is in fact buried in Tollcross Cemetery, in an unmarked grave), should have a portrait of the poet, but this has gone. What remains is a sturdy cenotaph with a lute and the inscription:

TO THE MEMORY OF
WILLIAM MILLER
"THE LAUREATE OF THE NURSERY"
AUTHOR OF "WEE WILLIE WINKIE"

Miller, born in the Briggate not far from here and brought up in what was then the village of Parkhead, was a skilled wood-turner, illness having thwarted his ambition to become a surgeon. Evidently he wrote as he worked, for among his manuscripts, held in the Mitchell Library, are some drafts of poems written on the smooth side pieces of sandpaper.

As we have seen, Miller was one of the contributors to the Whistle-Binkie anthologies. Such was his fame that there was a plaque on the now-demolished house, on the corner of George Street and Montrose Street, where his son Stephen lived. Stephen as a child was the hero of another of Miller's most popular poems, "The Wonderfu' Wean". It was Miller's near-contemporary Robert Buchanan who gave him the "Laureate" accolade, and since then the little gem "Wee Willie Winkie" has become known to millions who have no idea that its author was a Glasgow man.

Wee Willie Winkie
Rins through the toun
Upstairs and doon stairs
In his nicht-goun,
Tirlin' at the window,
Crying at the lock,
"Are the weans in their bed?
For noo it's ten o'clock"

William Miller the "Poet Laureate of the Nursery"
GLASGOW CITY LIBRARIES

"Wee Willie Winkie runs through the town" from *The Old Nursery Rhymes*
illustrated by Lawson Wood GLASGOW CITY LIBRARIES

The monument to another poet, William Motherwell, is also in a bad state of repair. Only the most determined enquirer can identify it now, for the stone slab bearing the inscription has split and fallen away. The carved friezes round the base can scarcely be made out, except on the more sheltered north side, facing the carriageway, where the two mounted knights engage in lively combat while followers and friends look on. There was originally a marble bust of the poet under the canopy of the little temple-shaped monument. Motherwell was born at 177 High Street, another house which has now been demolished, and educated in Paisley, where he became a sheriff-clerk and began to write verse. He moved into journalism, becoming editor of the *Paisley Advertiser*, and returned to Glasgow to edit the *Courier* there. Another of the Whistle-Binkie group, he continued to write and play a part in local politics until his early death.

William Motherwell by Andrew Henderson
SCOTTISH NATIONAL PORTRAIT GALLERY

Also buried in the Necropolis are Dugald Moore, a printer, bookseller and minor poet in the early nineteenth century, and Alexander Rodger, a contemporary and friend of Motherwell, whom we shall meet when we reach the East End.

The High Street, leading down from the Cathedral, was one of the four main streets of the early city which met at Glasgow Cross. For over four hundred years Glasgow University was situated here. The University was established by papal bull in 1451 (only St Andrews is older among Scottish universities, and only Oxford and Cambridge in England), and its presence, with its many distinguished students, has no doubt helped to encourage the literary life of Glasgow over the years.

University of Glasgow: principal entrance to the Old College from High Street, 1827
GLASGOW UNIVERSITY LIBRARY, DEPARTMENT OF SPECIAL COLLECTIONS

The University was originally based in the Cathedral, but soon moved to the High Street, where new premises - the "Old College" - were built about 1660. The fine complex of buildings, quadrangles and gardens, much admired by visitors to the city, was demolished in the nineteenth century when the University moved west to Gilmorehill, and only such names as College Street and the new development College Lands now mark the site. Though the move was probably inevitable, a model of the Old College to be seen in the present Hunterian Museum at the University shows us that much was lost. (Two fragments of the Old College are incorporated in the Gilmorehill buildings: the Lion and Unicorn staircase in Professors' Square, and part of the gatehouse, which forms the facade of the Pearce Lodge.)

Opposite the former site of the Old College, at 215 High Street, is an attractive red sandstone building bearing a plaque which announces:

ON THIS SITE
STOOD THE HOUSE
IN WHICH THE
POET CAMPBELL
LIVED

One writer on old Glasgow describes this as "a necessarily cautious statement", since the birthplace of Thomas Campbell was probably a little west of this. But the plaque, tucked away just round the corner of the building in narrow Nicholas Street, is particularly attractive, depicting a crowstepped old Glasgow house and a group of citizens in the street outside.

South of Glasgow Cross the High Street leads into the Saltmarket, another of Glasgow's ancient streets. Here, in a corner building known as Gibson's Land, long ago demolished, lived Tobias Smollett when he was an apothecary's apprentice. His largely autobiographical novel *Roderick Random* is said to caricature his boss Dr. Gordon as "Mr. Potion", a neighbouring and rival apothecary as "Mr. Launcelot Crab", and other then-notable Glasgow figures.

Close in Saltmarket, 1874
GLASGOW UNIVERSITY LIBRARY, DEPARTMENT OF SPECIAL COLLECTIONS

Tobias Smollett, portrait from *Smollett Works* GLASGOW CITY LIBRARIES

This part of Glasgow is Rob Roy country. The merchant Bailie Nicol Jarvie, whom we have already mentioned once or twice, lived here:

> ". . . I can win my crowns, and keep my crowns, and count my crowns, wi' ony body in the Saut-Market, or it may be in the Gallowgate."
>
> from *Rob Roy* by Walter Scott

If we move back up High Street (noting on the way that its steep upper part, the Bell o' the Brae, is mentioned in Blind Harry's epic poem "The Wallace"), we come to the Cathedral and its famous description by Andrew Fairservice:

> "Ah! it's a brave kirk - nane o' yere whigmaleeries and curliwurlies and open-steek hems about it - a' solid, weel-jointed mason-wark, that will stand as lang as the warld, keep hands and gunpowther aff it."
>
> from *Rob Roy* by Walter Scott

Leading young Francis Osbaldistane into the hallowed spot, Andrew proceeds to give a brief history of how the Cathedral survived the Reformation, and Francis is much impressed by the place, if a little distracted when the voice of Rob Roy - as he later discovers - whispers in his ear: "You are in danger in this city."

Bailie Nicol Jarvie from *Glasgow Today 1909*
by David Small
GLASGOW UNIVERSITY LIBRARY, DEPARTMENT OF SPECIAL COLLECTIONS

The powerful grouping of Cathedral and Necropolis has impressed itself on the minds and work of Glasgow writers much more recent than Scott. It appears in Alasdair Gray's *Lanark*, set partly in Glasgow and partly in the fantastic cities of Unthank and Provan, aspects of (perhaps) some nightmarish future Glasgow. It is from the Necropolis that Lanark descends into the sinister institute, and later his son is born in the Cathedral. An apocalyptic last chapter shows us "the whole landscape tilted like a board" as subsidence and flood threaten the Cathedral; but it survives.

⇢   ⇢   ⇢

DERICK S. THOMSON / RUARAIDH MAC THOMAIS

The Glasgow Connection

Gaelic writers have had quite a close association with Glasgow, especially over the last three centuries. The famous eighteenth-century poet Alasdair MacMhaighstir Alasdair attended the University in the early years of the century, and much Gaelic writing and publishing has been centred in Glasgow in the nineteenth and twentieth centuries. The Gaelic quarterly *Gairm* has appeared regularly for the last forty-two years, and its associated bookshop is visited by Gaelic enthusiasts from many countries. I have for long observed Glaswegians on the streets and in the cafes, and sometimes these impressions emerge as poems, especially about the less privileged or odder characters, of which Glasgow has a generous contingent.

Derick S. Thomson/Ruaraidh MacThòmais 1995

Derick S. Thomson/Ruaraidh MacThòmais was Professor of Celtic at the University of Glasgow from 1963 until 1991. An award-winning Gaelic poet, he founded *Gairm* magazine and has made Gaelic poetry of all periods his specialised subject. He was the first recipient of the Ossian Prize in 1974 and an early winner of the Saltire Scottish Book of the Year Award. His publications include *The Companion to Gaelic Scotland* (1987) and *Smeur An Dochais - The Bramble of Hope* (1992) .

EDWIN MORGAN

Fog City

Without being nostalgic about it, I have a strong recollection of the great Glasgow fogs of the decade after the Second World War. In the spruced-up city of today, these are now no more than memories, and no doubt thought of as a good riddance, but to a writer (or indeed any artist) dark cities can be as attractive as bright ones. At the end of the 1940s, Glasgow was still heavily industrialised, with many soot-blackened and grime-encrusted buildings, and with smoke pouring from thousands of coal-burning chimneys. It was also a city of unabashed and prolific smokers. And of course it is a northern city of early winter evenings. So its fogs could be spectacular. One night in 1947 or 1948 I was returning by train from London, and when I got into Central Station I could not understand why such a crowd of people was massed at the entrance. I soon found out why. Gordon Street was a silent wall of impenetrable grey. There were no buses, trams, taxis or cars to be seen or heard. It was a stricken, immobile place. No-one could get home. I booked a room in the Central Hotel, and as I slipped between the sheets I reflected it was the first time I had stayed at a hotel in my own town: an experience! These fogs penetrated everywhere; in the cinemas each film looked like *Quai des brumes*, and the Golden Divans in Green's Playhouse were more than usually seductive. The long cinema queues of those pre-booking days, snaking round whole blocks, huddled together as if afraid some segment might break off and be lost for ever. We did not curse the fog: it was simply one recurring phase of the environment. Half-sinister, half-romantic nocturnal wanderings by the River Kelvin seemed incomplete unless the nose-prickling waves of an oncoming fog combined with the acrid but haunting smell of the scummy effluent on the water to fix a future memory unmodified by anything politically correct.

Edwin Morgan 1995

Edwin Morgan was born in Glasgow in 1920 and educated at Rutherglen Academy, Glasgow High School and the University of Glasgow. He was appointed Titular Professor of English at Glasgow University in 1975, a post he held for the next five years. An award-winning poet, critic and translator, his many publications include *Poems of Thirty Years* (1982), *Collected Poems* which was published in 1990 to mark his 70th Birthday and *Sweeping Out the Dark* (1994), a celebration of 21 years of his poems, prose and translations. *Nothing Not Giving Messages* (1990), a reflection of his life and work was edited by Hamish Whyte and Robert Crawford and published to coincide with his 70th birthday.

The East End

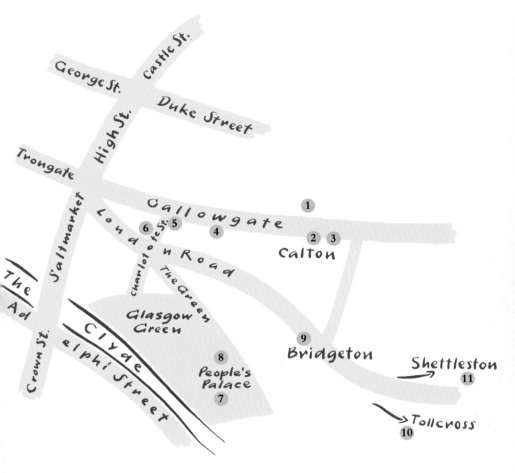

1. Saracen's Head Inn – Robert Burns, Boswell &
   Johnson, Dorothy & William Wordsworth
2. James Macfarlan
3. Matt McGinn
4. Cliff Hanley
5. John Gibson Lockhart
6. Alexander Smith
7. Hugh Macdonald
8. Robert & Andrew Foulis:
   Alasdair Gray's series of portraits
9. Alexander Rodger
10. Jack House
11. J. J. Lavin

Our tour of the East End of Glasgow begins in the Gallowgate, another of the four ancient streets

Muslin Street, Bridgeton by John Quinton Pringle CITY ART CENTRE, EDINBURGH

25

leading from Glasgow Cross. Here is the Saracen's Head, still a notable Glasgow pub (popularly known as the Sarry Heid), but of particular interest to us because the original Saracen's Head, on the same site, was the first hotel in Glasgow, established in 1755. A large and informative signboard on the side of the present building, in Saracen Head Lane, tells us the story. The inn was built (from the ruins of the old bishop's palace) on the site of Little St Mungo's Church, and St Mungo's Well was in its courtyard. The legend that St Mungo (officially known as Kentigern) and St Columba met here has been wittily explored by Edwin Morgan:

> God but le son du cor, Columba sighed
> to Kentigern, est triste au fond silvarum!
> . . .Veni venator sings the gallus kern
> The saints dip startled cups in Mungo's well
> > from "Colloquy in Glaschu" in *Sonnets from Scotland,* 1984

It is rather more certain that Burns may have stayed at the Saracen's Head as did Johnson and Boswell in 1773. "Adam Smith was ejected", the signboard informs us, "after a swearing-match with Dr. Johnson, whom he called a son of a bitch". William and Dorothy Wordsworth stayed here in 1803, no bad language being reported from them. The present Saracen's Head keeps some memorabilia from these earlier days, though one very striking item, as we shall see, is now in the People's Palace.

We are now in the Calton, once a weavers' village, and birthplace in slightly more recent years of several Glasgow writers. James Macfarlan is one of the most interesting. A contemporary describes him: "Of slender form, tattered garments, and commonplace features, he seemed every inch the gaberlunzie" (that is, beggar or tramp; Macfarlan is sometimes called the Pedlar Poet). Another writer concurs, and indeed goes further, but he frames the description with an enconium.

> If ever a human being breathed in whom the divine fire burned with unquenchable flame,
> that man was the ragged, unkempt, mean-looking tramp, who from dingy garrets and
> common lodging-houses in the slums of Glasgow sent forth to the world such beautiful
> lyrics as "The Poet" [and] "The Ruined City". . .

Macfarlan, then, was a paradox in his own time, and remains so. He discovered poetry at the age of twelve (while on the road with his father, a weaver turned pedlar), and had himself written sufficient for a collection by his early twenties. These "City Songs" were well enough received, and some poems were accepted by Charles Dickens for publication in his magazine *All the Year Round*, but Macfarlan lived a wandering, hand-to-mouth existence, and there was usually a drink in his hand. He died of consumption, only thirty years old, in an attic in the Drygate slums.

About a hundred years later another poet was born in the Calton, the singer and songwriter Matt McGinn. (Once following Lord MacLeod of Fuinary in signing a

Matt McGinn GLASGOW MUSEUMS THE PEOPLE'S PALACE

visitors' book, he capped the signature "MacLeod of Fuinary" with "McGinn of the Calton".) He grew up in the disturbed conditions of World War II and spent two years in an approved school, a time unsparingly depicted in his novel *Fry the Little Fishes*. In his early thirties he went to Oxford on a Trade Union scholarship, returning to Glasgow as the folk-song movement of the 1960s was reaching its height. As writer and performer of contemporary folk-songs - humorous, angry and tender by turns - he was a much-loved figure on the Glasgow scene.

Cliff Hanley from
Natural Light Portraits of Scottish Writers ANGELA CATLIN

Gallowgate was the birthplace of Cliff Hanley, whose autobiographical *Dancing in the Streets* immediately took its place as a Glasgow classic.

> It is so ludicrous to imagine anybody actually building the things that I have always assumed that Glasgow's tenements have just always been there...When I first read about the ancient Picts running about in woad and scaring the life out of Caesar's Legions, I took it for granted that they did their running about through the closes and back courts of Gallowgate...

Since then Hanley has been a prolific writer of both novels and non-fiction works, many of them set in or descriptive of the city which he so evidently loves.

Very few houses now remain in Charlotte Street, leading south off Gallowgate, once a highly fashionable address (at the south end) and a respectable street of tenements for artisans (at the north). John Gibson Lockhart, son-in-law and biographer of Walter Scott, lived at no. 40, now demolished. A house nearer the north end of the street was the family home of Alexander Smith; as a child and young man he lived on the top floor with his parents and five brothers and sisters. Smith, "a trembling windflower of a child", as he tells us in "A Boy's Poem", had a hard time when he started school, but found solace in the city scape seen from the Charlotte Street attic;

> What joy, when o'er the huddled chimney-tops
> Rose the great yellow moon!

John Gibson Lockhart with Charlotte Sophia Lockhart by Robert Scott Lauder SCOTTISH NATIONAL PORTRAIT GALLERY

This house has gone, but a similar one next door at no. 24 has (at the time of writing) survived, a tall old tenement oddly graceful in its isolation.

Charlotte Street leads us straight into Glasgow Green, the city's treasured and traditional open space. It has been in its time fairground, drying-green, venue for meetings and demonstrations, and much more, and as we shall see, has given rise to a great deal of Glasgow writing. At present we shall only note, just south of the People's Palace, a memorial fountain to Hugh Macdonald inscribed with the opening lines of his poem "The Bonnie Wee Well". As befits the author of *Rambles Round Glasgow*, he will appear again more than once.

The People's Palace, an inexhaustible store of Glasgow history, has several examples of the fine printed books produced by Robert and Andrew Foulis. The brothers were accustomed, we are told, to hang up the sheets of a work in the University, after their always-meticulous proofreading, and offer a reward of £50 to anyone who found an error. That was a small fortune in the eighteenth century, but, seeing the immaculate pages on display, we may guess that it was not often claimed.

There is a copy too of the first Glasgow newspaper, founded in 1715 as the *Glasgow Courant*, though by its fourth issue, which the People's Palace holds, it had been renamed *West Country Intelligence*. We may also admire the massive hand-printing press used in the late eighteenth century to produce the *Advertiser*, forerunner of the *Glasgow Herald*.

Prominently on view among other eighteenth-century momentos is a five-gallon punchbowl from the Saracen's Head, which must have seen a few lively nights in its time. (In fact it has acquired several nasty cracks on some such occasion, though it has been thriftily repaired and used again.) The bowl may have been made in one of the Glasgow potteries like Delftfield, long since gone; certainly it bears the motto "Success to the Town of Glascow" and a naturalistic rendering of the city's coat of arms including an uncommonly large salmon.

Just as interesting, though not always on display, is a collection of paintings and drawings carried out in 1977 by Alasdair Gray. He was employed for a year under a Job Creation Scheme to produce a series of works showing contemporary Glasgow and Glasgow people. Of the thirty portraits, nine are of writers: Tom McGrath, Alex Scott, Liz Lochhead, James Kelman, Tom Leonard, Archie Hind, Cliff Hanley, Edwin Morgan and Jack House (all of whom we shall meet in the course of this tour). In their various settings - a pub, an industrial landscape, a west-end flat - they are a marvellous snapshot of one moment in the literary history of Glasgow.

A little farther east is Bridgeton, another former weaving community. Here lived Alexander Rodger, sometimes called "the Radical Poet" (though we may feel, looking at Glasgow poets past and present, that he is not exactly alone in meriting that description). He was born in Midlothian but came to Glasgow about the age of twelve, and was apprenticed to a weaver. He also taught music to support his family, and later became a cloth-inspector at Barrowfield printworks. Later still he spent some time as a pawnbroker, but soon regretted the change:

O dark and dreary be that doleful day,
When to this sink of sin seduced away,
He turned on blythesome Barrowfield his back...

Alexander Rodger "the Radical Poet" from a copy of "Whistle-Binkie" GLASGOW CITY LIBARIES

Meanwhile he was writing satirical and political verse, and got into trouble through his association with radical journalism, being arrested at one point and jailed for eleven days. (He beguiled his time in prison by singing his own compositions at the top of his voice.) In calmer times, after his stint in the pawnbroker's, he returned to journalism and worked on several Glasgow papers. He was, as we have seen, one of the Whistle-Binkie group, and progressed to editing later volumes in the series.

Bridgeton was the birthplace of Hugh Macdonald, whose memorial we have noted on Glasgow Green. He was apprenticed as a block-printer, and, like many young city men, spent his spare time walking in the countryside. Having begun to write poetry and prose, he became a sub-editor of the *Glasgow Citizen*. There, with James Hedderwick as editor, he was able to encourage other writers and to contribute his own series, "Rambles Round Glasgow" and "Days at the Coast", later published in book form. The Glasgow Green fountain was in fact transferred there from the Gleniffer Braes above Paisley, a favourite ramble of his.

Hugh Macdonald from *Rambles round Glasgow* GLASGOW CITY LIBRARIES

Shettleston and Tollcross, beyond Bridgeton, also have their literary connections. The journalist and local historian Jack House, regarded for years as "Mr. Glasgow", was puckishly pleased to reveal in his later life that he wasn't a Glasgow man at all. He was born in 1906 in Tollcross, which did not become part of Glasgow until 1912. However, he surmounted this handicap and became a most readable and respected authority on every aspect of Glasgow history and life. He published over seventy books, and in 1988 he was awarded the prestigious St Mungo Prize, given every three years to the person judged to have done most for the city.

Jack House "Mr. Glasgow" from *Pavement in the Sun* GLASGOW CITY LIBRARIES

Glasgow Green, and the East End in general, have powerfully fired the imagination of Glasgow writers. There is some recognition of the early days when the toffs lived here. In Guy McCrone's *Wax Fruit*, old Mrs Barrowfield still lives in Monteith Row, "that had, when she was yet a growing girl, been built to be the most exclusive terrace of Regency Glasgow". But even then Glasgow was moving west as factories sprang up around the Green. Hugh Macdonald in the early 1850s can still observe that

Few towns can boast such a spacious and beautiful public park as the Green of Glasgow, with its widespreading lawns, its picturesque groups of trees, its farwinding walks, its numerous delicious springs, and, above all, its rich command of scenery. The 'lungs of

London' may exceed it in extent of surface and in artificial adornment, but in beauty of situation and variety of prospect our own Green certainly surpasses any of the street-girt metropolitan breathing-places. The Green of Glasgow lies to the south-east of the City, on the north bank of the Clyde, which, in a fine bold sweep, forms its southern boundary. It embraces in all about 140 imperial acres, and is surrounded by a carriage-drive two and a-half miles in length, besides being intersected in every direction by gravelled walks, overhung, in some instances, by the foliage of stately trees, which forms a pleasant screen from the noonday sun or the pelting shower; while every here and there seats have been erected for the convenience of the weary lounger.

from *Macdonald's Rambles,* 1851-52

but not many years later David Pae looks beyond the grass and trees:

Across, on the south side of the river, and far down by its eastern bank, and away verging to the north, were tall chimneys and long blocks of high square buildings, with many rows of windows, which flashed back the beams of the sinking orb of day. . . These were the cotton factories and other large works which give such character and importance to Glasgow. . . Encircled by these noisy factories was the Green and the river. . .

from *The Factory Girl,* 1868

Pae was a prolific novelist and editor of the popular *People's Friend;* much of his writing appeared in serial form there and in similar periodicals. While this quote is from his novel *The Factory Girl,* we should note that a real factory girl, Ellen Johnston, was writing poems and an autobiography about this time. She gives us a rare glimpse of a working-class woman's life in Victorian Glasgow, though she died in her thirties in the Barony poorhouse.

Much more recent poets have responded to the strangeness of the Green where beauty and ugliness can meet. Iain Hamilton's "News of the World" begins in calm ballad mode:

As I came round by Templeton's
The sun was sliding low,
And every spire round Glasgow Green
Gave off its godly glow. . .

Deep in its rut the river shed
A skin of shit and scum,
And glinted through the fretted bridge,
Gold as Byzantium.

Then suddenly the sun was snuffed
Behind a sooty cloud,
And night let fall on Glasgow Green
Its sulphur-stinking shroud. . .

but fear and violence supervene, until

In a black night of black despair
From Glasgow Green I go.

from "News of the World", 1949

And so often, Edwin Morgan encapsulates the place and its feelings:

> . . . the dirty starless river
> is the real Clyde, with a dishrag dawn
> it rinses the horrors of the night
> but cannot make them clean,
> though washing blows
>   where the women watch
> by day,
>   and children,
>   on Glasgow Green.
>
> . . . Let the women sit in the Green
> and rock their prams as the sheets
> blow and whip in the sunlight.
> But the beds of married love
> are islands in a sea of desire.
> Its waves break here, in this park,
> splashing the flesh as it trembles
> like driftwood through the dark.

from "Glasgow Green", 1963

Some of the finest Glasgow novels have their roots in the East End. The novelist J. J. Lavin was brought up in Shettleston and used the area as a background for his writing. As well as some short stories, he published a single novel, *Compass of Youth*, the story of a boy growing up in Shettleston. Almost forgotten now, it is a vivid and powerful book which ought to be rediscovered.

A much better-known novelist Robin Jenkins, important in the wider picture of Scottish literature, sets several of his novels in Glasgow. *Guests of War* treats the clash of lives and cultures when Glasgow mothers and children were evacuated to the countryside during World War II. *A Very Scotch Affair* is a bitter picture of narrowness and betrayal. Mungo Niven is a despicable character, but is the east-end "ghetto" of his upbringing partly to blame? Jenkins, as in all his work, is much too thoughtful and complex a writer to answer yes or no.

Robin Jenkins at the 1993 Edinburgh Book Festival DOUGLAS ROBERTSON

George Friel could be considered at several points of our tour - he was brought up in Maryhill, where he set *Grace and Miss Partridge* - but *Mr. Alfred MA*, probably his masterpiece, begins in the East End. In the grim streets and grimmer schools of Tordoch (Friel supplies a spoof Gaelic derivation which probably identifies the area as Blackhill) Mr. Alfred, a middle-aged bachelor schoolteacher, slips towards disgrace and alcoholism. Friel spent his working life as a teacher, publishing only a handful of short stories and five novels. The two mentioned above at least, and perhaps *The Boy Who Wanted Peace*, are outstanding works of fiction, perceptive in observation, complex in construction and language. Undervalued for years, Friel has at last been recognised as a major Glasgow writer.

31

J.F.Hendry, like Lavin, traces a boy's development in his one novel *Fernie Brae*. St Rollox with its once-famous locomotive works is the background to David's childhood, though he is in touch too with his mother's family home in Pollokshaws. As he grows up he explores the whole of Glasgow before he leaves for America and

> . . . the vast hand of the sea reached up and wiped away the inarticulate map of the fighting city. . .

Archie Hind's character Mat Craig stays in the fighting city and struggles with inarticulacy. He is a writer, striving to capture the life around him; it isn't easy, for writing is (or so it appears) alien to his family and class.

> "Writing! [his mother yells]
> You've nae time to think of
> things like that. You've got
> a wife and wean depending
> on you."

At the end of this novel, *The Dear Green Place*, Mat is in despair; but wonderfully, the voicing of his dilemma here seems to have set Glasgow writers free. *The Dear Green Place* is now seen as seminally important in the great surge of contemporary Glasgow writing - Alasdair Gray, Tom Leonard, James Kelman are only three names in the roll-call - which gathered force in the 1960s, swept forward in the 1970s and 1980s and is far from over yet.

Archie Hind from *Natural Light Portraits of Scottish Writers*
ANGELA CATLIN

⇢   ⇢   ⇢

LIZ LOCHHEAD

The Bargain

The river in January is fast and high.
You and I
are off to the Barrows
Gathering police-horses twitch and fret
at the Tron end of London Road and Gallowgate.
The early kick-off we forgot
has us, three thirty, rubbing the wrong way
against all the ugly losers
getting ready to let fly
where the two rivers meet.

January, and we're
looking back, looking forward,
don't know which way

but the boy
with three beautiful Bakelite
Bush radios for sale in Meadow's Minimarket is
buttonpopping stationhopping he
don't miss a beat sings along it's easy
to every changing tune.

Yes today we're in love aren't we?
with the whole splintering city
its big quick river wintry bridges
its brazen black Victorian heart.
So what if every other tenement
wears its hearth on its gable end
all I want

is my glad eye to catch
a glint in your flinty Northern face again
just once. Oh I know its cold
and coming down
and no we never lingered long among
the Shipbank traders.
Paddy's Market underneath the arches
stank too much today
the usual wetdog reek rising
from piles of old damp clothes.

from Dreaming Frankenstein Polygon (1984)

Liz Lochhead was born in
Motherwell in 1947. After
graduating from Glasgow
School of Art, she combined
writing with teaching for a
number of years, before
becoming a full-time writer.
She is an award-winning poet
and playwright and spends a
great deal of her time travelling
and giving performances of her
work. The publication of
Dreaming Frankenstein and
Collected Poems (1984) brought
her previous work together to
provide a complete collection
of her poetry from 1967 to
1984. Her plays include *Mary
Queen of Scots Got her Head
Chopped Off* and an
adaption/translation of *Tartuffe*.

The City Centre

1. Glasgow Herald Building
2. John Smith & Son
3. Bret Harte
4. Thomas De Quincey
5. School of Art: Stephen Mulrine,
   John Byrne, Alasdair Gray, Liz Lochhead
6. Catherine Carswell
7. Mitchell Library
8. Willow Tea Rooms: Kate Cranston
9. Blythswood Square: Madeleine Smith, Oscar Slater

The term City Centre is a fairly elastic one in Glasgow, but we shall just use it here to mean the grid of streets between Buchanan Street and, roughly, Charing Cross: the area where traditionally the city's main businesses, shops, theatres and cinemas were to be found, though this is no longer entirely true.

Glasgow School of Art Library DOUGLAS CORRANCE

35

In Buchanan Street, for instance, we may admire the former Glasgow Herald building at no. 65, while noting that the paper itself has moved east to Albion Street. On plaques at first-floor level we see *putti*, little plump boys, carrying out various printing processes and reading the result of their work; the third is hauling away at the handle of a printing press like the one we have seen in the People's Palace. The fathers of printing, Caxton and Gutenberg, stand on the top floor. (It is worth going round into narrow Mitchell Street to see the back of the building with its unexpected 150-foot tower, in the design of which Charles Rennie Mackintosh is thought to have had a hand.) *The Herald* - as it is now simply called - is the oldest national newspaper in the English-speaking world, having been founded (as *The Advertiser*) in 1783, two years before *The Times* of London.

Not far away at 57 St Vincent Street is the main bookshop of John Smith and Son. The present fine building dates from about 1850, but the firm was founded in 1751. By 1787 it was important enough for Burns to write to his publisher arranging for the

Glasgow Herald Building 1894
© HUNTERIAN ART GALLERY, UNIVERSITY OF GLASGOW: MACKINTOSH COLLECTION

second edition of his poems to be sold there. West Regent Street, a little farther north, has two odd literary connections. No. 107 was once the US Consulate in Glasgow, and the American novelist Bret Harte was Consul there during the years 1880-1885. Harte lived in the (now-demolished) Grand Hotel at Charing Cross, and several of his stories from this period have Glasgow settings or references.

Thomas De Quincey by Sir John Watson Gordon
SCOTTISH NATIONAL PORTRAIT GALLERY

At the corner of Renfield Street and West Regent Street is a building called De Quincey House. Thomas De Quincey, author of *Confessions of an English Opium Eater*, came to Glasgow several times during the 1840s, lodging in Rottenrow and High Street as well as in the former building on this site. One Glasgow historian informs us that this particular lodging was in fact rented to house his books while he stayed elsewhere, a surely ideal solution to the bookworm's perennial problem.

Thomas De Quincey - his fame, during his life, spread by his eccentricity as much as his literary achievements - by the end of his life was consuming 80,000 drops of laudanum per day rendering many details of his life in Glasgow unrecorded and perhaps best forgotten. To one of his long-suffering landladies:

"Madame, owing to dyspepsia affecting my system, the possibility is that additional derangement of the stomach might take place and consequences incalculably distressing arise - so much so indeed as to increase nervous irritations and prevent me from attending to matters of overwhelming importance - if you do not remember to cut the mutton in a diagonal rather than longitudinal form."

North of Sauchiehall Street is Garnethill, crowned by the School of Art, Charles Rennie Mackintosh's masterpiece. No visitor should miss it, but it is of particular interest because of its connections with several distinguished Glasgow writers. The poet and dramatist Stephen Mulrine, for instance, has been a lecturer here for some years, and John Byrne is well regarded as both painter and dramatist.

Alasdair Gray, whose novel *Lanark* we have already mentioned, studied here (as does his character Duncan Thaw in the "realistic" sections of *Lanark*). For some years Gray lived by painting - portraits, murals and scene-painting - as we have seen in our tour of the People's Palace. Most notably, he designs and illustrates his own books, so that each one is a stunning visual as well as literary experience.

John Byrne Self-portrait in Stetson
GLASGOW MUSEUMS: GALLERY OF MODERN ART

Liz Lochhead also graduated from the School of Art, teaching for some years before she became a full-time writer. First recognised as a poet, she moved through raps and performance pieces to the drama which is currently her main field. To all these forms she brings sharp observation, wit and the female perspective, counterbalancing the "hard man" image of some Glasgow literature. Much of her work contains Glasgow and West of Scotland references, though her concerns are far from being purely local.

Alasdair Gray DOUGLAS ROBERTSON

Liz Lochhead from
Natural Light Portraits of Scottish Writers ANGELA CATLIN

Except that there is a rail station called Anderston, it would nowadays be easy to miss the district of that name, since it is bisected by a ring road and the approaches to the Kingston Bridge. Two old burying-grounds in this area had interesting literary connections. A friend of Burns, Alexander Findlater, was buried in the cemetery known as North and South Woodside in North Street, demolished when the ring road was being built. Findlater was an exciseman in Dumfries and later in Glasgow. In the burying-ground of St Mark's Church in Cheapside Street, also now demolished, was a memorial stone to the poet James Macfarlan, whose short and sad life we have noted earlier. Fourteen poets and artists followed his body to the Cheapside Street cemetery, and a historian tells us that

> as they lowered the body into the grave the scene was lit up by a flash of vivid lightning, and a rolling peal of thunder crashed out overhead. The heavens gave the poet his requiem.

Near the top of North Street stands the Mitchell Library, Glasgow's central reference library. It was founded under the will of Stephen Mitchell, a wealthy tobacco manufacturer, and opened in 1877 in a building at the corner of Ingram Street and Albion Street. As its stock grew the library moved in 1891 to premises in Miller Street, and than in 1911 to the present building in North Street. It was extended in 1953, and then, when the adjacent St Andrew's Halls burned down in 1962, a major extension on the vacant site was planned. This opened in 1980, and the Mitchell, with a stock of more than one million items, is the largest public reference library in Europe. It is divided into self-contained subject departments - Arts, Science and Technology, and others - and no book about Glasgow, certainly not this one would see the light without the services of its renowned Glasgow Room. The Rare Books and Manuscripts department of the Mitchell holds manuscripts of many local writers.

→ → →

Catherine Carswell describes Garnethill with an accurate eye in the early chapters of her semi-autobiographical novel *Open the Door!*

> Collessie Street [a fictional name], at the top of its precipitous, roughly cobbled hill, had at one time been a residential quarter of distinction. But in 1896, the roomy, solid black houses - deep-bitten by the carbonic deposits of half a century - with their square-pillared porticoes, and their stone areas guarded by rusty spear-head railings, had a forsaken look.

Carswell, whose two novels are both set at least partly in Glasgow, was also a biographer and critic, and a friend of D.H.Lawrence, who encouraged her in the writing of *Open the Door!* (She lost her job with the *Glasgow Herald* after writing a favourable review of his then-banned novel *The Rainbow.*) *Open the Door!* is, for its time, strikingly honest and strong, and Carswell is now seen as a key figure in Scottish women's writing.

Catherine Carswell from Lying Awake An Unfinished Autobiography GLASGOW CITY LIBRARIES

The Centre for Contemporary Arts in Sauchiehall Street was once the Third Eye Centre, founded in the early 1970s. (The third eye, as Zen aficionados will know, is in the middle of the forehead and sees things not visible to the physical eye.) It has remained a vibrant part of the Glasgow arts scene. An early director of the Third Eye was Tom McGrath, a poet and dramatist, notable for - among much other exciting work - *The Hard Man*, a play based on the experiences of Jimmy Boyle while serving a life sentence for murder.

Also in Sauchiehall Street, the Willow Tearooms, designed by Charles Rennie Mackintosh for the Glasgow restaurateur Kate Cranston, have been restored and brought back into use in recent years. They still contain some of the original fittings of Mackintosh's Room De Luxe, and so we can appreciate a contemporary description:

> The chairs is no' like ony other chairs ever I clapped eyes on, but ye could easy guess they were chairs; and a' roond the place there's a lump o' lookin'-gless wi' purple leeks painted on it every noo and then.

This is from the sketch "Erchie in an Art Tea-Room" by Neil Munro, who (writing as Hugh Foulis) produced a long series of such pieces for the *Glasgow Evening News*. His *Erchie* and *Jimmy Swan* sketches are set in and around Glasgow, though he is better known for his Highland

Mackintosh Ladies' Luncheon Room popularly known as the White Dining Room from Miss Cranston's Ingram Street Tea Rooms GLASGOW MUSEUMS

sketches featuring Para Handy and the crew of the *Vital Spark*. Under his own name Munro wrote historical novels with the background of his native Inveraray in Argyll, which are worth rediscovering, having been undervalued for some time.

Anderston, though not named as such, is the setting for Robert Nicholson's *Mrs. Ross* and *A Flight of Steps*, Glasgow novels which should be better known than they are. (Mrs. Ross

"Erchie" by Neil Munro
GLASGOW CITY LIBRARIES
& DONALD WARD

Neil Munro
by William Strang
SCOTTISH NATIONAL PORTRAIT GALLERY

was filmed under the title *The Whisperers*, but the story, for some reason, was moved to the north of England.) Their period is the 1960s, when Anderston - like so many areas of Glasgow - was largely disappearing before the approach of the ring road. The old woman Mrs. Ross, just slightly out of touch with reality, clinging stubbornly to the life she knows, is observed with compassion and flashes of gentle humour.

The Charing Cross area has the unusual distinction of being known as "The Square Mile of Murder", a name coined by Jack House. Four notable Glasgow murders occurred here in a space of some fifty years, between 1857 and 1909.

At 7 Blythswood Square Madeleine Smith poisoned her lover Pierre Emile L'Angelier by lacing his cocoa with arsenic (or so most people believe, though the verdict at her trial was the uniquely Scottish one of Not Proven). At 131 Sauchiehall Street, Dr. Edward Pritchard definitely

did poison his wife and her mother-in-law, thus becoming the last man in Glasgow to be hanged in public. At 17 Sandyford Place, Jessie McLachlan almost certainly did not murder her friend Jess McPherson, but was found guilty and condemned to death, a sentence fortunately commuted to life imprisonment.

Madeleine Smith & Emile L'Angelier from *The Trial of Madeleine Smith* GLASGOW UNIVERSITY LIBRARY, DEPARTMENT OF SPECIAL COLLECTIONS

Miss Smith and friends leaving the court from *The Trial of Madeleine Smith* GLASGOW UNIVERSITY LIBRARY, DEPARTMENT OF SPECIAL COLLECTIONS

View of the house and Madeleine Smith handing a cup of chocolate from her bedroom window to L'Angelier from *The Trial of Madeleine Smith* GLASGOW UNIVERSITY LIBRARY, DEPARTMENT OF SPECIAL COLLECTIONS

Oscar Slater "The Man Who Didn't" from *The Square Mile of Murder* by Jack House
GLASGOW CITY LIBRARIES

Most intriguing of all is the case of Oscar Slater, who was found guilty and condemned, though later reprieved and later still pardoned, for murdering Miss Marion Gilchrist at 15 Queen's Terrace (now 49 West Princes Street), a crime with which he had no connection at all. Naturally these cases have attracted the attention of novelists. Frank Kuppner's *A Very Quiet Street*

A Sketch of the Proceedings in the Slater Case from the Pen of an *Evening Times* Artist on May 4th 1909 from *The Square Mile of Murder* by Jack House GLASGOW CITY LIBRARIES

(subtitled "a novel of sorts") is a particularly fascinating treatment of the Oscar Slater case. Kuppner, a poet and prose writer, was brought up in West Princes Street next door to Miss Gilchrist's house, and interweaves his own memories with the story of the crime.

Whether by coincidence or otherwise, Glasgow authors have gone on to make a strong showing in crime fiction. W. Murdoch Duncan and Bill Knox are popular writers in the genre. Peter Turnbull sets his police procedurals in the fictitious P Division with its headquarters at Charing Cross. Edward Boyd wrote intricate thrillers, and in the 1970s scripted *The View from Daniel Pike*, an all-too-short television series about a Glasgow private eye. More recently, the long-running *Taggart*, with Glasgow settings and actors, has carried the tradition to a world-wide audience.

William McIlvanney's Detective-Inspector Laidlaw must also be mentioned here. McIlvanney, a novelist of great distinction, moves between Glasgow and "Graithnock" (his home town of Kilmarnock) in much of his fiction, but bases his crime fiction firmly in Glasgow. There have so far been three books, beginning with *Laidlaw* in 1982, about this unconventional, complex character, who oftens feels more kinship with the crooks than with his colleagues, and operates in a realistic yet haunting contemporary Glasgow:

> It was Glasgow on a Friday night, the city of the stare . . . Cities may all say essentially the same thing but the intonations are different. He was trying to re-attune himself to Glasgow's.

William McIlvanney DOUGLAS ROBERTSON

→ → →

CLIFF HANLEY

Partick

To the casual observer, the Partick district of Glasgow is just a mile or so of Dumbarton Road, flanked by tenements with shops on their ground floors. Quite 20th century.

In fact, it comes from a long way back. In the 6th century, it was the royal town of Perdyc, or Perk Inch (perk being a park and inch an island). It was visited by King David, and the natives were quite nice to him, even if they thought he sounded a bit foreign.

We find today few residents who are into that ancient lore. The locals are tuned into the present (especially at Christmas, of course) and they are full of good humour to any strangers present.

Cliff Hanley 1995

Cliff Hanley's writing career spans more than forty years. The autobiographical account of his Glasgow childhood *Dancing in the Streets* was first published in 1958 and is still in print today. Other books *The Taste of too much* (1960) and *Another Street, Another Dance* (1983) were also Glasgow-based. His working life began in journalism and he has written for radio, theatre and television. Using the pseudonym Henry Calvin, he has also written a number of popular thrillers.

Byres Road Pubs

"Ladies don't go into pubs." That dictum, along with "Never eat peas from your knife" and "Don't wipe your nose on your sleeve" was with me throughout childhood. As soon as student days took me to the big city of Glasgow, "Ladies don't go into pubs" was the first dictum I chose to ignore.

Being a student in Glasgow in the sixties and haunting, as students still do, Byres Road, there were plenty of pubs to choose from. Particular favourites then were The Curlers, The Rubaiyat, and The Aragon. The Curlers was noisy and busy and the "in" place to be. The Rubaiyat and The Aragon were always full of medical students let loose from the Western Infirmary. All the pubs served good beer, or so I was told. My pocket only ever stretched to a half pint shandy so it was difficult to be sure.

My daughter, now also a student in Glasgow, has been given no such dictum about pubs, though I believe I may have mentioned the inadvisability of peas on knives and snot on sleeves. She agrees that the three pubs I mentioned are still as good as ever and adds a further three.

The Living Room: Mega trendy. Full of thirty somethings chatting each other up. Good vodka.

Whistler's Mother: Nice cafe section. Good food and great coffee.

Jinty McGinty's: Great atmosphere. Superb Guinness.

But, the burning question. Did going into Byres Road pubs as a student influence my subsequent literary career? Hard to say. But those half pint shandies certainly made my writing wobbly.

Margaret Ryan 1995

Margaret Ryan has written numerous books for children including such well-known titles as *Millie Morgan Pirate* (1992), *Fergus the Forgetful* (1992) and *Puffling in a Pickle* (1995). She has produced articles for newspapers and magazines and several of her children's stories have been adapted for television and radio.

West and North

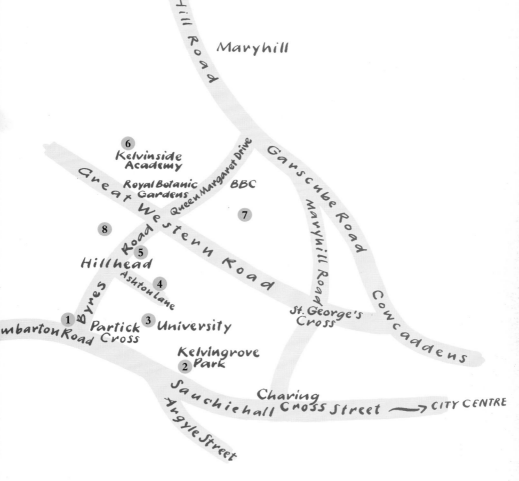

1. Duck Club: William Reid
2. Kelvingrove Park: Thomas Carlyle
3. University: Hamish Whyte,
   Edwin Morgan, Derick Thomson
4. Ubiquitous Chip: Alasdair Gray murals
5. Curlers Tavern: mural of Hugh MacDiarmid
6. J. J. Bell
7. Dot Allan
8. "The Writing Morrisons"

While the West End of Glasgow is, especially in the eyes of estate agents, as elastic a term as the City Centre, we shall look at the vastly varied area stretching roughly from Charing Cross west

Glasgow University by Night DONALD CLEMENTS

to Milngavie and from Partick north to Maryhill. Partick, an ancient settlement which held out as an independent burgh until 1912, was the location of the Duck Club, formed in the early nineteenth century for the laudable purpose of dining on the ducks which bred on the river Kelvin. The club's bard was William Reid, whom we have mentioned earlier in connection with Burns. He was a bookseller and publisher whose shop, as we have noted, was an early-meeting place for Glasgow writers. A historian describes his motto as "Laugh and grow fat", adding that "he never troubled himself about either his own obesity or that of anyone else who might follow his laughing example".

Kelvingrove Park, as we shall see, has inspired poets, though its only statue with much literary relevance is the stern bust of the prose writer Thomas Carlyle. Like Scott and Burns, Carlyle has probably been commemorated on the grounds of his general literary fame rather than for any particular Glasgow connection, but he did visit the city several times:

> I well remember the first visit, and pieces of the others; probably there were three or even four in all; each of them a real holiday to me!

The park provides a pleasant setting for Glasgow University, which, like its predecessor the Old College, has over the years housed and educated more writers than can be enumerated here. Hamish Whyte has described the University in the 1960s and 1970s as being "stuffed with poets" (including himself). During these stirring years, in fact, three major Glasgow poets were lecturing here.

Alexander Scott was the first lecturer in Scottish literature in Glasgow - and in Scotland - and in 1971 became Head of the Department of Scottish Literature, again the first such post in Scotland. He wrote poetry in both Scots and English, and was also a dramatist and critic, publishing a notable biography of the poet William Soutar.

Edwin Morgan lectured at the University for over thirty years, becoming Titular Professor of English. He is probably the city's greatest contemporary poet. His poetry is notable for its range of interests - "from Glasgow to Saturn", the title of a 1973 collection - and for its variety of form,

Edwin Morgan, Poet & Professor by Alasdair Gray GLASGOW MUSEUMS THE PEOPLE'S PALACE

from sonnets to concrete poems. He covers Glasgow, science fiction, love, the Middle East and current affairs with perception and wit. He is also a critic and translator of note.

Derick Thomson (Ruaraidh MacThòmais) was Professor of Celtic Studies from 1963 to 1991. He writes in Gaelic, often supplying his own English translations of his poems. He has done much to support and preserve Gaelic literature, including founding (in 1951) and editing the magazine *Gairm*.

Byres Road has some claim to be described as Glasgow's current literary quarter. Geographically it links the University and the Glasgow headquarters of BBC Scotland in Queen Margaret Drive. Socially it is noted for its pubs and restaurants, two at least of which have literary connections.

The Ubiquitous Chip in Ashton Lane contains vivid murals painted by Alasdair Gray in the years before he found fame as a novelist with *Lanark*.

And in the Curlers' Tavern in Byres Road, still occupying its original eighteenth-century building which used to front a curling pond, his murals feature celebrated customers of the past, among whom can be seen Hugh MacDiarmid (Christopher Murray Grieve). Though we cannot fairly describe MacDiarmid as a Glasgow poet – his roots were elsewhere and his fame is international – he did spend some time in Glasgow in the 1930s and 1940s. They were not particularly happy years and his view of Glasgow is not enthusiastic:

A terrible shadow descended like dust over my thoughts
Almost like reading a Glasgow Herald leader . . .

Many authors past and present have lived in this area of Glasgow. J.J.Bell was brought up in Bank Street and educated at Kelvinside Academy; he studied chemistry at Glasgow University before turning to journalism. His best-known work *Wee Macgregor,* began life as as series of sketches in the *Glasgow Evening Times,* and Bell had to guarantee £50 against possible loss before it was published in book form. It met with immediate success.

Because of contractual difficulties, however, Bell did not make a fortune with *Wee Macgreegor*. To earn a living he wrote many other books - probably too many - which did not quite recapture the charm of his first. But *Wee Macgreegor,* a humorous, observant, if slightly sentimental, picture of a very real wee boy in a working-class family, became, and has remained, a Glasgow classic.

Dot Allan, now an almost forgotten novelist though well regarded in her time, was born in Stirlingshire but lived for most of her life in the West End of Glasgow, working as a freelance journalist. She treated the shipping trade in her novels *The Syrens* and *Deepening River*, and women's life, a theme little handled in Glasgow fiction at that time, in the thoughtful *Makeshift*. Most striking is *Hunger March*, a novel of strong social concern covering one day in the depression years of the 1930s.

Wee Macgreegor GLASGOW MUSEUMS THE PEOPLE'S PALACE

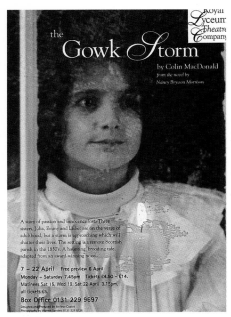

the
Gowk Storm

by Colin MacDonald

from the novel by Nancy Brysson Morrison

A story of passion and innocence lost. Three sisters, Julia, Emmy and Lisbet are on the verge of adulthood, but a storm is approaching which will shatter their lives. The setting is a remote Scottish parish in the 1850's. A haunting, brooding tale, adapted from an award-winning novel.

7 – 22 April   Free preview 6 April
Monday – Saturday 7.45pm Tickets £4.50 – £14.
Matinees Sat 15, Wed 19, Sat 22 April 3.15pm,
all tickets £5.
Box Office 0131 229 9697
Designed and Produced by McIlroy Coates
Photography by Warren Sanders 0131 221 6106

Programme cover from the Lyceum Theatre's 1995
production of *The Gowk Storm* by
Nancy Brysson Morrison
ROYAL LYCEUM EDINBURGH. McILROY COATES & WARREN SANDERS

Nancy Brysson Morrison
GLASGOW CITY LIBRARIES

West End literary life from about the 1930s to the 1950s was graced by a family known as "the writing Morrisons". All five brothers and sisters wrote, most notably perhaps Nancy Brysson Morrison, whose work is currently being rediscovered with the reissue of her sensitive novel *The Gowk Storm*. Her sister Peggy, who wrote as March Cost, also published several novels and was regarded as a fine prose stylist.

And contemporary writers are still associated with the area, like Bernard MacLaverty, originally from Belfast, whose fine novels and short stories examine the question of Northern Ireland with unequalled power and compassion, and Carl MacDougall, also a short story writer and a prose poet of Glasgow, who has mapped in his novel *The Lights Below* the destruction, in industrial and human terms, of his native district of Springburn.

⇢   ⇢   ⇢

Partick, or thereabouts, is the setting for mysterious events in one of the greatest of Scottish novels.

> I hurried through the city and sought again the private path through the field and wood of Finnieston. . . Near one of the stiles, I perceived a young man sitting in a devout posture reading on a Bible.
>
> from *The Private Memoirs and Confessions of a Justified Sinner* by James Hogg

Finnieston is just adjacent to Partick, and here Robert Wringhim meets Gil-Martin (for the second time, in fact, but Gil-Martin has completely changed his appearance since their previous meeting the day before) in James Hogg's *The Private Memoirs and Confessions of a Justified Sinner.* Hogg, of course, was a Borderer, and the events of the book take place largely in Edinburgh; why the Devil turns up in Glasgow is perhaps for literary scholars, satanists or Partick enthusiasts to explain.

Somewhere in this area too - at least, he was brought up in Drumchapel and his wife wants to move to Knightswood - lives Rab Hines in James Kelman's first novel *The Busconductor Hines*. But Kelman, indisputably a great Glasgow writer and now being recognised in national and international terms, cannot be pinned to one district. His novels and short stories, wherever they are set, speak the language of the city and give a voice to its sometimes inarticulate people. It is hard to imagine that he did not achieve book publication in Britain until 1983; now he is a central figure in Scottish literature and has inspired a whole group of younger urban writers.

As we move up through Kelvingrove Park, there is a temptation (as quite often in Glasgow) to quote William McGonagall, the bard of Dundee, who was "treated like a prince" when he visited Glasgow in 1889, and repaid the compliments with interest.

James Kelman DOUGLAS ROBERTSON

> Then as for Kelvin Grove, it is most lovely to be seen
> With its beautiful flowers and trees so green,
> And a magnificent water-fountain spouting up very high,
> Where people can quench their thirst when they feel dry.

from "Glasgow", 1889

Or we may burst into song:

> Let us haste to Kelvin Grove, bonnie lassie O!,
> Through its mazes let us rove, bonnie lassie O!,
>   Where the rose in all her pride
>   Paints the hollow dingle side,
> Where the midnight fairies glide, bonnie lassie O!.

William McGonagall from *Poetic Gems*
by William McGonagall
GLASGOW CITY LIBRARIES

> Let us wander by the mill, bonnie lassie O!,
> To the cove beside the rill, bonnie lassie, O,
>   Where the glens rebound the call
>   Of the roaring waters' fall
> Through the mountain's rocky hall, bonnie lassie, O.

> O! Kelvin banks are fair, bonnie lassie, O.
> When in summer we are there, bonnie lassie, O.
>   There the May-pink's crimson plume,
>   Throws a soft but sweet perfume
> Rounds the yellow banks of broom, bonnie lassie, O.

from "Kelvin Grove" by Thomas Lyle in
The Glasgow Poets: Their Lives and Poems
by George Eyre-Todd

This nineteenth-century versifier is now usually identified as Thomas Lyle, a Paisley man who practised medicine in Glasgow for some years.

Just as hard to forget, once heard, is James Bridie's serenade:

> Open your window the nicht is beastly derk,
> The phentoms are dencing in the West-End Perk,
> (an alternative name for Kelvingrove)
> Open your window, your lover brave to see,
> I'm here all alone, and there's no-one here but me!

It is sung, as can be seen, in the much-mocked Kelvinside accent, somewhat different from the everyday voice of Glasgow. In this area we have a bewildering variety of literary references. We may inspect the bridge over the Kelvin in Gibson Street where the eponymous villain (or is he?) of Frederic Lindsay's *Brond* threw a little boy to his death (or did our hero imagine it all?) Lindsay's fine novels, most with a Glasgow setting or connection, have the haunting quality of nightmare. *Jill Rips* is a treatment of the Jack the Ripper story exploring an underworld recognisable, though not named, as Maryhill.

Quite different are the stately terraces along the Great Western Road where Guy McCrone's Moorhouse family live in the pleasant ambience of the Victorian West End. McCrone is best remembered for his trilogy *Wax Fruit*, which continues the story of the Moorhouse and Hayburn families. Much knowledge and understanding of middle-class Victorian Glasgow has gone into these novels, and his businessmen, their wives and children come to life in books as rich as plumcake.

AL Kennedy DAVID THOMPSON   *Janice Galloway* DOUGLAS ROBERTSON

In Hyndland railway station nearby we may think of AL Kennedy's short story collection *Night Geometry and the Garscadden Trains*, but to confine Kennedy to one area of Glasgow - as in the case of Kelman - would be to undervalue her achievement. Since *Night Geometry* was published in 1990, Kennedy has shown herself to be a most complex and sensitive writer, whose novels and short stories demand to be read and reread. In *So I Am Glad* we find an out-of-time Cyrano de Bergerac appearing in a bedsitter house somewhere in this area. You never know who you're going to meet in Partick. And it is in University Avenue, waiting for a bus, that the young woman in Janice Galloway's short story "Frostbite" meets an old man who destroys conventional ideas:

What right had he? What right had any of them? She'd show him. She'd show the whole bloody lot of them. . . To hell with this waiting. There were other ways, other things to do.

It is an encounter emblematic of Galloway's fierce beautiful fiction, similarly not anchored in any specific place or time.

We must not miss one of the more recent and most delightful of Glasgow's literary monuments, to be found in Woodlands Road. It is a statue of Lobey Dosser, the Sheriff of Calton Creek, on his two-legged horse El Fideldo, with Rank Bajin (the villain, obviously) perched on the saddle behind him. Lobey Dosser, the creation of the cartoonist Bud Neill, appeared as a comic strip in the *Evening Times* from 1949 until 1955. So fondly was the deadpan, surreal quality of the strip remembered by readers that, thirty-five years later, a campaign by the Herald columnist Tom Shields raised most of the £18,000 cost of the statue, which was erected in 1992.

"Awfy clever wean' this. Say 'Awa an bile yir heid' that ye learnt aff the budgie, hen…"

A cartoon by *Bud Neill* in the 1950s
RANALD McCALL

Lobey Dosser, creation of the cartoonist *Bud Neill.* DOUGLAS ROBERTSON

The Clyde

Paper Boats by George Wyllie GEORGE WYLLIE

"The Clyde made Glasgow and Glasgow made the Clyde", and it is largely this process - the deepening of the Clyde so that ships could come upriver, and the consequent industrialisation - which has caught the imagination of Glasgow writers. Some poets have deplored the change, like Thomas Campbell:

> And call they this improvement? - to have changed,
> My native Clyde, thy once romantic shore,
> Where Nature's face is banish'd and estranged,
> And heaven reflected in thy wave no more;
> Whose banks, that sweeten'd May-day's breath before,
> Lie sere and leafless now in summer's beam,
> With sooty exhalations cover'd o'er;
> And for the daisied green-sward, down thy stream
> Unsightly brick-lanes smoke, and clanking engines gleam.
>
> from "Lines on Revisiting a Scottish River", 1827

Broomielaw, 1834 by J.Scott from *Glasgow Illustrated* GLASGOW CITY LIBRARIES

and Marion Bernstein:

> I'll sing a song of Glasgow town,
> That stands on either side
> The river that was once so fair,
> The much insulted Clyde.
> That stream, once pure, but now so foul,
> Was never made to be
> A sewer, just to bear away
> The refuse to the sea.
> Oh, when will Glasgow's factories
> Cease to pollute its tide,
> And let the Glasgow people see
> The beauty of the Clyde!

from "A Song of Glasgow Town", 1876

However, McGonagall had no problem with the busy river:

> 'Tis beautiful to see the ships passing to and fro,
> Laden with goods for the high and the low;
> So let the beautiful city of Glasgow flourish,
> And may the inhabitants always find food their bodies to nourish.

from "Glasgow", 1889

and Alexander Smith frankly celebrates it:

> The steamer left the black and oozy wharves,
> And floated down between dark ranks of masts.
>   . . . We slowly passed
> Loud building-yards, where every slip contained
> A mighty vessel with a hundred men
> Battering its iron sides. A cheer! a ship
> In a gay flutter of innumerous flags
> Slid gaily to her home.

from "A Boy's Poem", 1857

That was the scene in 1857. For many years after that, of course, the "loud building-yards" were the pride of the Clyde. Their story, their workers and their eventual decline gave rise to some fine Glasgow novels, like Dot Allan's *Deepening River*, already mentioned, which traces the development of Clyde shipbuilding from the eighteenth century until just before World War I.

Best known, perhaps, is George Blake's *The Shipbuilders*. Blake later criticised himself for "the adoption of a middle-class attitude to the theme of industrial conflict and despair", but the book is still full of gripping Glasgow scenes - an Old Firm football match, a High Court murder trial - and Blake's pictures of the idle shipyards, above all, remain in the reader's mind.

In contrast, James Barke's *Major Operation* was recognised on publication as an outstanding "proletarian novel". Barke had a country upbringing before settling in the Glasgow area - his family's odyssey is mirrored in his best novel *The Land of the Leal* and maintained throughout his

George Blake with Neil Gunn and Douglas Young by Emilio Coia
SCOTTISH NATIONAL PORTRAIT GALLERY

life a fierce concern for the underdog, whether in a rural or an urban setting. *Major Operation* brings together, in a hospital ward, a businessman and a shipyard workers' leader, whose opposing points of view can thus be presented and discussed. Apart from this, the book is notable for its many brief sketches of Glasgow life, full of colour, anger and an odd poetry.

These are only a few instances, for the Clyde, so central to the map of Glasgow, is also inescapable in Glasgow writing. It appears in the context of holidays "doon the watter" - Sarah Tytler's *St Mungo's City*, already mentioned, has a lively chapter on a Victorian steamer trip - of trade and industry, as we have seen, and of post-industrialism, unforgettably encapsulated by Edwin Morgan:

> . . . the great sick Clyde shivers in its bed.
> But elegists can't hang themselves on fled-
> from trees or poison a recycled cup-
> If only a less faint, shaky sunup
> glimmered through the skeletal shop and shed
>
> from "Glasgow Sonnet VI"

Morgan, indeed, looks into the city's future in his sonnet "Clydegrad":

> . . . Ziggurat-stark
> a power-house reflected in the lead
> of the old twilight river leapt alive
> lit up at every window, and a boat
> of students rowed past, slid from black to red
> into the blaze. But where will they arrive
> with all, boat, city, earth, like them, afloat?

Perhaps this is really the literary heart of Glasgow. It is not so surprising then that there is, in fact, poetry to be found in the Clyde. As you walk (or travel by bus) across Jamaica Bridge, look to your right to see lines by the poet Ian Hamilton Finlay incised on two massive piers remaining from an earlier, now-demolished, railway bridge.

55

PAT GERBER

A River runs through it

The Glasgow in which I was born is a city of rivers and green spaces. These are what I crave because my early life was spent roaming the moors of Renfrewshire, and later I reared my young among the soft rains of Argyll.

I have several "thinking" places in and around Glasgow, where I go to hatch plots, dream up weird and wonderous ideas for stories, plays and books, and often sorrowfully to abort the sillier of these. Today, I'm wandering along Clydeside from the helicopter terminal, shielded from traffic by the trees. On a summer's day I'll head downriver on the old paddle steamer Waverley. Later, sailing homeward up the last sunbeam, and the river shining like gold, it's easy to forget the pollution.

Other rivers flow in; the Cart and the Kelvin, both still needing to clean up their acts. When I began to write I'd go walking along the Kelvin, but now the place I go most often is Rouken Glen, where the Cart tumbles somewhat odoriferously over a fault-line into a wild woody glen that seems miles away from the town.

My writing is mostly set in Scotland's countryside, probably because it's all about dreaming and wish-fulfilment. But if I have to be a city-dweller, then I belong to Glasgow. The helicopter roars, and as it lifts from its pad I see my Glasgow as a city of the 21st century, taking care to leave room for everyone to enjoy its waterways and green places.

Pat Gerber 1995

Pat Gerber is a short story and non-fiction writer whose recent publications include *Maiden Voyage* (1992) and *The Search for the Stone of Destiny* (1992). She is also an experienced teacher of creative writing and lectures in the Department of Adult Education at Glasgow University. Her plays include *Edith, the Railway Child* and *Dancing, A Portrait of Margaret Morris*.

DAVID KINLOCH

Home

At school, our English teacher asked us to write about "home" in the manner of *Under Milk Wood*. It was an imaginative and daunting task, particularly when confronted by the imposing Victorian villas of Pollokshields. The French have a much better word - pavillon - for such bastions of merchant wealth, its vowels and consonants diluting, masking the raw entrepreneurial graft and occasional rape that laid their foundations in the late nineteenth century.

There is nothing quaint and proletarian about Pollokshields but its peccadillos are treated with as much secrecy ("discretion" would be the "district's" term) as in Dylan Thomas' Welsh village.

Pollokshields is substantially, grandly suburban, a curious mixture of hilly avenues, parks, classical facades and then, suddenly, round a corner, the gothic pile of a banker's steamy imagination. And that mixture was reflected in the impression Pollokshields made on my own childhood. It was a place of solid, bourgeois security lit unexpectedly by terrifying incursions from other planets like Govan: the day a gang of rougher, attractively well-built boys invaded on bikes and tried to hi-jack my own moulton-mini led gang, leaving me with a black eye and - unquenchably - in love. Having a "sprinkler" planted in my hair at a fireworks party on a broad midnight lawn, then douking for apples with the fork Gwen took from her lips.

What did suburban Glasgow leave me? A need to break taboos, a suspicion of - and occasionally a thankfulness for - gentility.

David Kinloch 1995

David Kinloch is a poet who writes in Scots and English. With Robert Crawford, he founded and edited *Verse* magazine. They also jointly published a book on the work of Douglas Dunn *Reading Douglas Dunn* (1992). He lectures in French at the Unversity of Strathclyde and other publications include *Dustie-Fute* (1992) and *Paris Forfar* (1994).

South Side

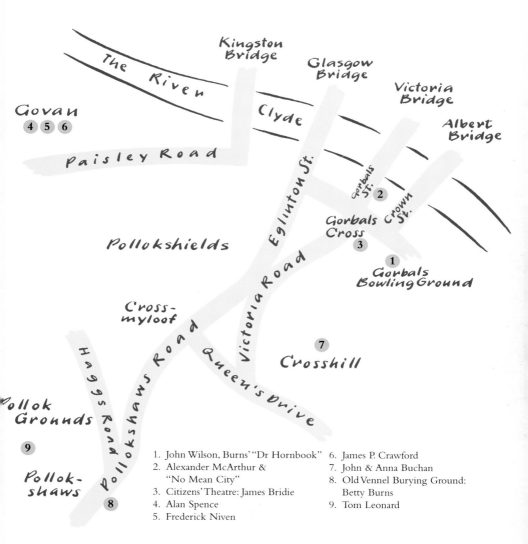

1. John Wilson, Burns' "Dr Hornbook"
2. Alexander McArthur & "No Mean City"
3. Citizens' Theatre: James Bridie
4. Alan Spence
5. Frederick Niven
6. James P. Crawford
7. John & Anna Buchan
8. Old Vennel Burying Ground: Betty Burns
9. Tom Leonard

To many thousands of people who know Glasgow only slightly, the South Side means Gorbals and Gorbals means *No Mean City*. Of course this is very wide of the mark. The various districts (once villages) of the South Side have their own long history and some unexpected literary connections. The Southern Necropolis, for instance, contains not only the grave of Hugh

A close in the Gorbals from Edward Gaiten's *Dance of the Apprentices* Illustration by William Maclellan GLASGOW CITY LIBRARIES

Macdonald but that of John Begg, a nephew of Burns. In the old Gorbals burial ground is a stone to "John Wilson, session-clerk of Gorbals". He moved here from Tarbolton in Ayrshire, where, as schoolmaster and amateur doctor, he was the model for Burns' Dr. Hornbook.

But we have to consider *No Mean City*, for many years, as it seemed, the only writing about Glasgow (with the possible exception of Robert McLeish's play *The Gorbals Story*) which the wider world had ever heard of. It's hard to think of another single novel which has brought about such a strong perception of a city; a perception strenuously rubbished at the time, and outdated now, but still around for all that.

Alexander McArthur

Alexander McArthur was an unemployed baker in Gorbals, who filled his idle hours by writing and bombarded publishers with his work. Nothing was accepted, because (so far as we can tell now) the books were so badly written as to be unpublishable. At last, however, the firm of Longmans, Green saw something in the content, if not the style, of McArthur's latest novel. So striking was the content in fact, that they suspected he had loaded it with squalor, sex and violence for the sake of effect. They made enquiries and interviewed McArthur, and, satisfied, employed a freelance journalist, H. Kingsley Long, to knock the sprawling manuscript into shape. The result was *No Mean City*.

The arguments began at once and have gone on ever since. At first they centred on McArthur and Long's highly-coloured picture of a slummy Gorbals riven by gang wars and ruled by Razor King. Gorbals people complained that it wasn't their Gorbals, a neighbourly and much-loved place in spite of its poor housing conditions. Non-Gorbals Glaswegians protested that even if Gorbals was like that, Kelvinside (or Pollokshields or Hyndland. . .) certainly was not. The reading public revelled in *No Mean City*, which is still in print some sixty years after its first publication, and a legend was born.

Later critics have attacked not so much the content (which is, after all, not so very shocking now) but the style. *No Mean City*, in this view, is pulp fiction and beneath consideration. When Alasdair Gray writes in *Lanark* "imaginatively Glasgow exists as a music-hall song and a few bad novels", it's a safe guess which particular bad novel first springs to mind.

Recently it has been possible to take a more balanced view of *No Mean City*; to see that it did speak out with strength and directness if with minimal literary skill, and to ask why it has had such a lasting effect. The *No Mean City* debate probably has some mileage in it yet.

But other and better writers have come from Gorbals and used it as a setting for their work. The powerful, sensitive short stories of Edward Gaitens were collected in *Growing Up*. His better-known novel *Dance of the Apprentices* draws on them for several of its chapters, including the "famous Macdonnel party" which begins when

> Jimmy, home from the sea, comes. . . stumbling happily up the street with his Aunt Kate's hat on his head and his arm round his father's neck. They were lustily singing "The Bonny Lass o' Ballochmyle". . . Behind them, laughing like witches, came Mrs. Macdonnel and

Aunt Kate with the Sailor's cap on, followed by six of Jimmy's pals who were carrying between them three large crates of bottled beer...

The irresistible humour of the following bacchanalia blends with the conflicting emotions it arouses in young Eddy Macdonnel, whose growing up is the theme of both books.

More recently Jeff Torrington has won praise and the Whitbread Prize for *Swing Hammer Swing!*

Something really weird was happening in the Gorbals - from the battered hulk of the Planet Cinema in Scobie Street, a deepsea diver was emerging. He hesitated, bamboozled maybe by the shimmering fathoms of light, the towering rockfaces of the snow-coraled tenements. . . .

Poetry and humour overlap in this vivid book, set in the 1960s when Gorbals was literally being knocked down and rebuilt. This process still continues, for Gorbals is an ever-changing place.

And unexpectedly, a few yards from Gorbals Cross (as it is still officially called, though McArthur and Gaitens would never recognise it), we find the internationally recognised Glasgow Citizens' Theatre. Shakespeare and Burns greet the visitor in the foyer - they are two of the six statues which used to adorn the theatre's facade, now more safely housed inside - and on the back wall there is a modest bronze plaque with a portrait medallion.

OSBORNE HENRY MAVOR

(JAMES BRIDIE)

OBE, LLD, MD, FRFRS(G)

PHYSICIAN AND DRAMATIST

1888-1951

FOUNDER OF THE CITIZENS THEATRE

James Bridie and Sonia Dresdel SCOTTISH THEATRE ARCHIVE

A scene from the 1950 Edinburgh Festival production by Glasgow Citizens' of James Bridie's *The Queen's Comedy* with Sonia Dresdel as Juno and Stanley Baxter as Mercury. SCOTTISH THEATRE ARCHIVE

Bridie's witty and thoughtful plays were popular on the London west-end stage from the 1930s onwards - it was 1938 before he gave up his medical practice to become a full-time writer - and still merit critical attention. He was also a founder of the College of Drama in what is now the Royal Scottish Academy of Music and Drama, and, during his student days, of Glasgow University Magazine and the annual student extravaganza Daft Friday, but perhaps his founding of the Citizens' Theatre was his major gift to Glasgow.

Alan Spence from *Natural Light, Portraits of Scottish Writers* ANGELA CAITLIN

Almost as rich in literary connections is Govan, another historic former burgh and more recently a centre of Clyde shipbuilding; it can probably be identified as the "shipbuilding parish" in which Frederick Niven's *Mrs. Barry* is set. Alan Spence grew up in Govan and his story sequence *Its Colours They Are Fine* traces the childhood and adolescence of a group of young boys against this background. The stories darken in tone from innocence to mindless violence as, with economy and compassion, Spence focuses on the experiences which shape his characters in ways they cannot recognise at the time.

A nineteenth-century Glasgow writer equally moved by social problems was James P. Crawford, a tailor who later became registrar of the Parish Board of Govan. The source of most of the misery he encountered there was clear to him as he wrote his poem "The Drunkard's Raggit Wean". The title became a household word and the poem was immensely popular for many years as a temperance recitation.

> A wee bit raggit laddie gangs wan'rin' through the street,
> Wadin' 'mang the snaw wi' his wee hackit feet,
> Shiverin' i' the cauld blast, greetin' wi' the pain-
> Wha's the puir wee callan? He's a drunkard's raggit wean.
>
> He stan's at ilka door, an' keeks wi' wistfu' e'e
> To see the crowd aroun' the fire a' laughin' loud wi' glee;
> But he daurna venture ben, though his heart be e'er sae fain,
> For he mauna play wi' ither bairns, the drunkard's raggit wean.
>
> Oh, see the wee bit bairnie, his heart is unco' fu',
> The sleet is blawin' cauld, and he's droukit through and through;
> He's speerin' for his mither, an' he won'ers whare she's gaΔ3
> But oh! his mither, she forgets her puir wee raggit wean.

He kens nae faither's love, and he kens nae mither's care,
To soothe his wee bit sorrows, or kaim his tautit hair,
To kiss him when he waukens, or smooth his bed at e'en;
An' oh! he fears his faither's face, the drunkard's raggit wean.

Oh, pity the wee laddie, sae guileless an' sae young!
The oath that lea's the faither's lips 'll settle on his tongue,
An' sinfu' words his mither speaks his infant lips'll stain;
For oh! there's nane to guide the bairn, the drunkard's raggit wean.

Then surely we micht try an' turn that sinfu' mither's heart,
An' try to get his faither to act a faither's part,
An' mak' them lea' the drunkard's cup, an' never taste again,
An' cherish wi' a parents' care their puir wee raggit wean.

"The Drunkard's Raggit Wean" from
The Glasgow Poets: Their Lives and Poems edited by George Eyre-Todd

"O. Douglas" Anna Buchan from her autobiography
Unforgettable, Unforgotten A.P. WATT LTD. & EDINBURGH CITY LIBRARIES
Left: Sir John Buchan, 1st Baron Tweedsmuir by
Thomas John Clapperton SCOTTISH NATIONAL PORTRAIT GALLERY

But some South Side residents would not fail to point out that their area includes posh bits too. John Buchan and his sister Anna, who wrote as O. Douglas, lived in Crosshill for some years while their father was a minister there and attended the prestigious Hutcheson's Grammar School (as did Frederick Niven). O. Douglas's novel *The Setons* depicts the place and time:

"It was really written for my mother," she said, "an attempt to reconstruct for her our home-life in Glasgow".

John Buchan's *Huntingtower* features the Gorbals Die-Hards, based on "eight very bad small boys" whom he encountered while a Sunday School teacher in his father's church.

John Macnair Reid wrote two novels, *Homeward Journey* and the posthumously published *Judy from Crown Street*, which consider the social divide, very evident in his time, between Gorbals and Pollokshields. Reid, a journalist in Glasgow for some years, has another claim to be remembered in Scottish literature. He took Neil Gunn round the slums of 1930s Glasgow, and the result can be seen in *Wild Geese Overhead*, a city novel and as such something of a departure from Gunn's usual concerns.

Not to be confused with Pollokshields is Pollokshaws, immortalised in the Glasgow saying "There's queer folk in the Shaws". (No one really knows when and where this blithe description was first used, though it crops up in more than one nineteenth-century Glasgow poem.)

> Who ne'er unto the Shaws has been
> Has surely missed a treat:
> For wonders there are to be seen
> Which nothing else can beat.
>
> The folks are green, it's oft been said,
> Of that you'll find no trace:
> There's seasoned wood in every head,
> And brass in every face.
>
> Look smart, and keep your eyes about,
> Their tricks will make you grin;
> The Barrhead coach will take you out,
> The folks will take you in.

"Queer Folk at the Shaws"
by Jamie Blue (James McIndoe), c. 1820

One unexpected and rather exciting literary connection is to be found in Pollokshaws. In 1859 a dinner was held in Glasgow to celebrate Robert Burns' centenary, and, we are told by one of the guests,

A grandson of the poet was one of the party, a son of Mrs. Thomson, the daughter of Burns, who lived somewhere out by Crossmyloof or the Shaws.

Or some damn place like that, we can almost hear him add; we see that the practice of doorstepping the families of the famous was not yet in vogue, anyway not in Glasgow.

But a tombstone in the old burial ground in Pollokshaws, variously known as the Old Vennel or Kirk Lane burying ground, confirms the information.

R.B. THOMSON
TO HIS FATHER AND MOTHER
JOHN THOMSON, 85
AND BETTY BURNS, 83
DAUGHTER OF THE POET
ROBERT BURNS

Betty, who died in 1873, was not a daughter of Bonnie Jean's, but was born of an extra-marital liaison with Anna Park of Dumfries.

Ye Monarchs take the East and West
Frae Indus to Savannah!
Gie me within my straining grasp
The melting form of Anna.

from The Gowden Locks of Anna by Robert Burns

Nevertheless, as the tombstone shows, she rightly recognised her family connections; we may make a fairly safe guess at the forenames of her son R.B.Thomson. Also buried here, as well as the poet's nephew Gilbert Burns Begg, is another member of the family, James Glencairn Thomson, named for Burns' patron, the Earl of Glencairn.

Another name on the stone is that of "Margaret Thomson, widow of David Wingate". This was an alliance of poetic families. Wingate, son of a miner who died in a fire-damp explosion when the boy was five years old, went down the pit himself at the age of nine. He was one of the poets discovered by Hugh Macdonald and published in the *Glasgow Citizen*. His collections of poetry were successful enough to let him study for a certificate in colliery management, allowing him more time for writing in his later years.

Tom Leonard was brought up in Pollok and has written that, as a boy, Wingate was his favourite local poet. Leonard first came to notice in the 1960s with his poem "The Good Thief":

> heh jimmy
> yawright ih
> stull wayiz urryi
> ih. . .

Since then his poetry and prose, groundbreaking, committed, often angry, have become an important strand of current Glasgow writing, along with the work of Gray, Kelman and Lochhead.

Tom Leonard from *Natural Light Portraits of Scottish Writers* ANGELA CATLIN

Life in Govan and Gorbals has been chronicled by many writers besides those mentioned above, for instance in autobiographies by the novelists Evelyn Cowan and Christine Marion Fraser. We find that Pollokshaws, to J.F.Hendry's David in *Fernie Brae,* is another world entirely:

> It was the opposite of all Springburn stood for. It was old Scotland, a garden of gold bees and breasts of fruit, bright as a patch of sun in the drab life of these streets, and inspiration.

And a fictional treatment of Govan in the 1930s, *The Breadmakers,* opened the prolific writing career of Margaret Thomson Davis in style. It was the first book of a trilogy, and her very popular novels have since explored other areas of Glasgow in periods from the eighteenth century to the present day.

Gorbals in the early part of the twentieth century helped to shape the minds of two great Scottish writers not primarily associated with Glasgow. The poet Edwin Muir's family moved from Orkney to Glasgow when he was fourteen. Culture-shock and family tragedy combined to make Glasgow seem a nightmare place to Muir, as we see in both his semi-autobiographical novel *Poor Tom* and in his *Autobiography* itself:

> ...if I was tired or ill I often had the feeling, passing through Eglinton Street or Crown Street, that I was dangerously close to the ground, deep down in a place from which I might never be able to climb up again... though I lived in a decent house, the slums seemed to be everywhere around me, a great, spreading swamp into which I might sink for good.

The novelist Lewis Grassic Gibbon spent some years in Glasgow and regarded it in a later essay with no friendly eye:

Authors in Session Edwin Muir, James Bridie, Neil Gunn, Eric Linklater by Stanley Cursiter
GLASGOW MUSEUMS ART GALLERY & MUSEUM, KELVINGROVE

In Glasgow there are over a hundred and fifty thousand human beings living in such conditions as the most bitterly pressed primitive in Tierra del Fuego never visioned. They live five or six to the single room... it is a room that is part of some great sloven of tenement ... its windows grimed with the unceasing wash and drift of coal-dust, its stairs narrow and befouled and steep, its evening breath like that which might issue from the mouth of a lung-diseased beast ...

The attempt to get rid of these slums led to Glasgow's outlying housing-schemes like Castlemilk, Drumchapel and Easterhouse and to high-rise blocks of flats. These, a writer suggests, brought their own problems:

> I'm a skyscraper wean; I live on the nineteenth flair,
> But I'm no' gaun oot tae play ony mair,
> 'Cause since we moved tae Castlemilk, I'm wastin' away
> 'Cause I'm gettin' wan meal less every day:
>
> *Oh ye cannae fling pieces oot a twenty-storey flat,* ★
> *Seven hundred hungry weans'll testify to that.*
> *If it's butter, cheese or jeely, if the breid is plain or pan,*
> *The odds against it reaching earth are ninety-nine tae wan...*

from "The Jeely Piece Song", 1967

★as mothers were accustomed to do from tenement windows, nourishing their weans between meals with doorstep sandwiches.

This modern Glasgow classic, "The Jeely Piece Song", is by singer and songwriter Adam McNaughtan, who, having also explored and catalogued the nineteenth-century Poets' Box collection in the Mitchell Library, has contributed to the treasure-chest of Glasgow literature both old and new.

The Spirit of the Suburbs

My spirit country is the suburbs, Cambuslang in particular. When I grew up there in the 1960s and 1970s our road seemed so ordinary that I never saw a tourist on it. Now, when I go back, the streets round our old house are redolent of mid-century, middle-class Scotland. These solid sandstone villas are approaching their centenary, each house surrounded by a defensive middle-class leafiness - sycamores, monkey puzzle trees, firs with cones the size of pint glasses. Cambuslang's older streets show its social geology: below the Main Street was working class, above it middle class. From Stewarton Drive at the top of the hill, doctors and businessmen surveyed the lower strata. Gardening here was the main art form, and an expression of social virtue. Some of the big gardens in the zone above the Main Street are still rich in fruit and vegetables as ours was, though more and more are purely ornamental. Privacy and quiet are the watchwords here in an architecture of bourgeois reserve. Everything happens subcutaneously. To write about this area without mockery or aggrandizement is to try to articulate not the noisy public life of the often written about inner urban areas, but the quietly powerful suburbs where so many Glaswegians made and make their homes. Glasgow cannot be understood without its Cambuslangs. Walking along Brownside Road or Central Avenue you will notice suddenly the city's least photographed face.

Robert Crawford 1995

Robert Crawford was born in Bellshill in 1959. He teaches Modern Scottish Literature at St Andrews University and is a poet, editor, translator and critic. With Hamish Whyte, he edited a tribute to Edwin Morgan published to celebrate his 70th birthday and with Thom Nairn, a critical appreciation of the work of Alasdair Gray. In his own right, he has written books such as the award-winning *The Savage and the City in the work of T.S Eliot* (1987) and a book of poetry, *A Scottish Assembly* (1990).

Glasgow Authors and Booklist

This is a very selective bibliography and some of the books listed here will now be out-of-print but your local library will be able to help you.

Dot Allan (1892-1964), novelist
The Deans (1929)
Charity Begins at Home (1958)

James Barke (1905-58), novelist
Major Operation (1936)
The Land of the Leal (1939)

Henry Glassford Bell (1803-74), poet
Summer and Winter Hours (1831)
Romances and Minor Poems (1886)

J.J. Bell (1871-1934), novelist
Wee Macgreegor (1902)
Courtin' Christina (1913)
The Braw Baillie (1925)

Marion Bernstein (?1840-?), poet
Mirren's Musings (1876)

William Black (1841-98), novelist
White Heather (1885)

George Blake (1893-1961), novelist
The Shipbuilders (1935)
The Paying Guest (1949)
The Peacock Palace (1958)

Edward Boyd (1916-89), novelist and
  dramatist
The Dark Number (1973)
The View from Daniel Pyke (1974)

Zachary Boyd (1585-1653), preacher and
  poet
Zion's Flowers (1831)
The Last Battell of the Soule in Death (1831)

James Bridie (1888-1951), dramatist
The Anatomist (1931)
Mr Bolfry (1943)
Mr Gillie (1950)

Anna Buchan see O. Douglas

John Buchan (1875-1940), novelist
The Thirty Nine Steps (1915)
Mr Standfast (1919)
The Island of Sheep (1936)

Robert Buchanan (1841-1901), novelist
Idylls and Legends of Inverburn (1866)
The Book of Orm (1882)

Moira Burgess (b. 1936), novelist and
  bibliographer
The Day before Tomorrow (1971)
A Rumour of Strangers (1987)
The Glasgow Novel: a bibliography (1986)

John Burrowes, novelist
Incomers (1987)
Mother Glasgow (1991)

Thomas Campbell (1777-1844), poet
The Pleasures of Hope (1799)
Annals of Great Britain (1806)

Catherine Carswell (1879-1946), novelist
  and biographer
Open the Door! (1920)
The Camomile (1922)

Stewart Conn (b. 1936), poet and dramatist
The Burning (1973)
In the Kibble Palace (1987)
The Luncheon of the Boating Party (1991)

Left: A still from the BBC film *Boswell and Johnson's Tour of the Western Isles* starring Robbie Coltrane as Dr Samuel Johnson and John Sessions as his biographer James Boswell. The film was John Byrne's debut as a film director © BBC

March Cost (? – 1973), novelist
The Dark Glass (1935)
The Bespoken Mile (1950)

Evelyn Cowan (b. 1926), novelist
Spring Remembered: a Scottish Jewish Childhood
(1974)
Portrait of Alice (1976)

James P. Crawford (1825-87), poet
Author of 'The Drunkard's Raggit Wean';
no collections of his work published

Robert Crawford (b.1959), poet
A Scottish Assembly (1990)
Talkies (1992)

Margaret Thomson Davis (b. 1927),
novelist
The Breadmakers Trilogy (1972-3)
Hold Me Forever (1994)

O. Douglas (1877-1948), novelist
The Setons (1917)
Penny Plain (1920)
Unforgettable, Unforgotten (1945)

W. Murdoch Duncan (1909-75), crime
novelist
The Big Steal (1966)

Marcella Evaristi (b. 1953), dramatist
Wedding Belles and Green Grasses (1981)
Terrestrial Extras (1987)

Hugh Foulis see Neil Munro

Robert Foulis (1717-76) and
Andrew Foulis (1712-75), printers
Early Glasgow printers, most famous for
folio editions of the *Iliad* (1756) and the
Odyssey (1758)

Ronald Frame (b. 1953), novelist
Winter Journey (1984)
Bluette (1990)
The Sun on the Wall (1993)

Christine Marion Fraser (b. c. 1944), novelist
Rhanna (1978) and sequels
King's Croft (1986) and sequels

George Friel (1910-75), novelist
The Bank of Time (1959)
Grace and Miss Partridge (1969)
Mr Alfred M.A. (1972)

Edward Gaitens (1897-1966), novelist
Growing Up (1942)
Dance of the Apprentices (1948)

Janice Galloway (b. 1956), novelist
The Trick is to Keep Breathing (1990)
Blood (1991)
Foreign Parts (1994)

Pat Gerber non-fiction writer and
playwright
Maiden Voyage (1992)
The Search for the Stone of Destiny (1992)

William Glen (1789-1826), poet
The Lonely Isle (1816)
Reformiana (1817)

Alasdair Gray (b.1934), novelist
Lanark (1981)
1982, Janine (1984)
A History Maker (1994)

Iain Hamilton (1920-86), editor and poet
'News of the World'; worked at the *Daily
Record* 1944-5; later editor of the *Spectator*

Margaret Hamilton (1915-72), short story
writer and novelist
Bull's Penny (1950)

Cliff Hanley (b. 1922), journalist and novelist
The Taste of too much (1960)
Another Street, Another Dance (1983)

Chris Hannan (b. 1958), dramatist
The Orphan's Comedy (1986)
The Baby and The Evil Doers (1991)

James Hedderwick (1814–97), editor
Lays of Middle Age (1889)
Backward Glances (1891)

Iain Heggie (b. 1953), dramatist
American Bagpipes and other Plays (1989)

J.F. Hendry (1912–86), novelist and poet
Fernie Brae (1947)
Marimarusa (1978)
A World Alien (1980)

Archie Hind (b. 1928), novelist and dramatist
The Dear Green Place (1966)

Jack House (1906–91), journalist and local historian
Square Mile of Murder (1961)
The Heart of Glasgow (1965)
Pavement in the Sun (1967)

Robin Jenkins (b. 1912), novelist
The Conegatherers (1983)
Guests of War (1988)
Willie Hogg (1993)

Ellen Johnston (?1835–73), poet
Factory Girl's Poems (1869)

Jackie Kay (b. 1961), poet and dramatist
The Adoption Papers (1991)
Other Lovers (1993)

James Kelman (b. 1946), novelist
The Busconductor Hines (1984)
A Disaffection (1989)
How late it was, how late (1994)

A.L. Kennedy (b. 1965), novelist
Looking for the Possible Dance (1993)
So I am glad (1995)

David Kinloch (b. 1959), poet
Dustie-fute (1992)

Bill Knox (b. 1928), crime novelist
The Crossfire Killings (1986)
The Interface Man (1989)

Frank Kuppner (b.1951), poet and prose writer
Ridiculous! Absurd! Disgusting! (1989)
A Very Quiet Street (1989)
Something Very Like Murder (1994)

J.J. Lavin (1902–?68), novelist
Compass of Youth (1953)

Tom Leonard (b. 1944), poet
Intimate Voices (1984)
Reports from the present (1995)

Frederic Lindsay (b. 1933), novelist
Brond (1984)
Jill Rips (1987)

Maurice Lindsay (b. 1918), poet
The Advancing Day (1940)
This Business of Living (1969)
Thank you for having me (autobiography) (1983)

Liz Lochhead (b. 1947), poet and dramatist
Dreaming Frankenstein (1984)
Mary Queen of Scots got her Head Chopped Off (1989)

John Gibson Lockhart (1794–1854), novelist and editor
Peter's Letters to his Kinsfolk (1819)

Thomas Lyle (1792–1859), poet
'Kelvin Grove'; no collection of his work published

Alexander McArthur (1901–47), novelist
with H. Kingsley Long *No Mean City* (1935)
with Peter Watts *No Bad Money* (1969)

Guy McCrone (1898–1977), novelist
Wax Fruit (1947)
Aunt Bel (1949)
An Independent Young Man (1961)

Hugh Macdonald (1817–60), prose writer
Rambles around Glasgow (1854)
Days at the Coast (1860)

Carl MacDougall (b. 1941), novelist
Elvis is Dead (1986)
The Lights below (1993)

James Macfarlan (1832-62), poet
City Songs (1855)
Poetical Works (1882)

Matt McGinn (1928-77), singer and
  songwriter
Fry the little Fishes (1975)
McGinn of the Calton (1987)

Tom McGrath (b. 1940), poet and dramatist
The Hard Man (1977)
Animal (1979)

William McIlvanney (b. 1936), novelist
Remedy is None (1966)
Docherty (1975)
Strange Loyalties (1991)

Bernard MacLaverty (b. 1942), novelist
Cal (1983)
Walking the Dog and other Stories (1994)

Robert McLeish (1912 -), dramatist
The Gorbals Story (1946)

Hector MacMillan (b. 1929), dramatist
The Sash my Father Wore (1974)

Adam McNaughtan (b. 1939), singer and
  songwriter
Records/cassettes: *Words, Words, Words*
The Glasgow that I used to know

Ruaraidh MacThòmais see Derick Thomson

William Miller (1810-72), poet
Scottish Nursery Songs and Poems (1863)

Dugald Moore (1805-41), poet, printer and
  bookseller
The African (1829)
The Bard of the North (1833)

Edwin Morgan (b.1920), poet
The Second Life (1968)
Sonnets from Scotland (1984)
Hold Hands among the Atoms (1991)

Nancy Brysson Morrison (- 1986),
  novelist
The Gowk Storm (1933)
Thea (1963)

William Motherwell (1797-1835), poet
(ed) *The Harp of Renfrewshire* (1819)
Poems Narrative and Lyrical (1827)

Stephen Mulrine (b. 1937), poet and dramatist
Poems (1971)

Neil Munro (1864-1930), novelist
Erchie, my droll Friend (1904)
Jimmy Swan, the Joy Traveller (1917)
Para Handy and other Tales (1931)

Bud Neill (1911-70), cartoonist
Lobey's the Wee Boy! (compilation, 1992)

Robert Nicolson (1910-81), novelist
Mrs Ross (1961)
A Flight of Steps (1966)

Frederick Niven (1878-1944), novelist
The Justice of the Peace (1914)
The Staff at Simson's (1932)
The Transplanted (1944)

Agnes Owens (b. 1928), novelist
Gentlemen of the West (1984)
Like Birds in the Wilderness (1987)
A Working Mother (1994)

David Pae (1828-84), novelist and editor
The Factory Girl (1868)

Hugh C. Rae (b. 1935), novelist
Skinner (1965)
Night Pillow (1967)
as Jessica Stirling:
Treasures on Earth (trilogy 1985-7)
The Good Provider (quartet 1987-90)

John Macnair Reid (1895-1954), novelist
Homeward Journey (1934)
Judy from Crown Street (1970)

William Reid (1764-1831), bookseller
Poetry, original and selected (1795-8)

Alexander Rodger (1784-1846), poet
Peter Cornclips (1827)
Poems and Songs (1838)

Frank Rodgers, children's author and
 illustrator
B is for Book! (1992)
The Pirate and the Pig (1996)

Margaret Ryan, children's author
Millie Morgan Pirate (1992)
Puffling in a Pickle (1995)

Alexander Scott (1920-89), poet and
 dramatist
Cantrips (1968)
Greek fire (1971)

Tom Scott (b. 1918), poet
The Ship and ither Poems (1963)
At the shrine o' the unkent Sodger (1968)
The Tree (1977)

Alexander Smith (1827-67), poet and
 essayist
City Poems (1857)
A Summer in Skye (1866)

Tobias Smollett (1721-71), novelist
The Adventures of Roderick Random (1748)
The Expedition of Humphrey Clinker (1771)

Alan Spence (b.1947), novelist and dramatist
Its Colours They Are Fine (1977)
The Magic Flute (1990)

Jessica Stirling see Hugh C. Rae

Derick Thomson (b. 1921), poet
An Dealbh Briste (1951)
An Rathad Cian (1970)
Smeur An Dochais (1991)

Jeff Torrington (b. 1935), novelist
Swing, Hammer, Swing (1992)
The Devil's Carousel (1996)

Alexander Trocchi (1925-84), novelist
Young Adam (1954)
Cain's Book (1966)

Peter Turnbull (b. 1950), crime novelist
Deep and crisp and even (1981)
Fair Friday (1983)
The Killing Floor (1994)

Sarah Tytler (1827-1914), novelist
St Mungo's City (1885)

Joan Ure (1919-78), dramatist
Something in it for Ophelia (1971)
Take your old rib back, then (1974)

Brian Whittingham, poet
Ergonomic Workstations and Spinning Teacans (1992)
Industrial Deafness (1990)

Christopher Whyte (b. 1952), poet and
 novelist
Uirsgeul = Myth (1991)
Euphemia McFarrigle and the Laughing Virgin
 (1995)

Hamish Whyte (b.1947), poet and editor
Rooms (1986)
Mungo's Tongues (ed) (1993)

David Wingate (1828-92), poet
Annie Weir and other Poems (1866)
Lily Neil (1879)

Glasgow Bookshops

ADAM BOOKS
47 Parnie Street
Glasgow G1 5LU
Tel:0141-552-2665 Scottish & Secondhand Books

AKA BOOKS & COMICS
31-35 Parnie Street
Glasgow G1
Tel:0141-552-6692 Science-fiction & Horror Books

ASIAN BOOK CENTRE
177 Allison Street
Glasgow G42
Tel:0141-423-9440

BARGAIN BOOKS
11 Argyle Street
Glasgow G2 8AH Remainder Books

BARGAIN BOOKS
86 Gordon Street
Glasgow G2 8HE Remainder Books

BARGAIN BOOKS
74 Saucheihall Street
Glasgow G2 3AH Remainder Books

BARGAIN BOOKS
223 Byres Road
Glasgow G12 8UD Remainder Books

BASEMENT BOOKSHOP
Alba Cafe
61 Otago Street
Glasgow General Secondhand Books

BLACKWELL'S
83 St Vincent Street
Glasgow G2 5TF
Tel:0141-221-1369 Business & Law Books

BOOK PEDLAR
Unit 12, Shawlands Arcade
124 Kilmarnock Road
Glasgow G41
Tel:0141-636-6016 Remainder Books

BOOKPOINT
2 Churchill Way
Bishopbriggs
Glasgow G64 2RH
Tel:0141-762-3553 General Books

BOOKWORLD
St Enoch Centre
Glasgow G1 4BW General & Remainder Books

CALEDONIA BOOKS
483 Great Western Road
Glasgow G12 8HL
Tel:0141-334-9663 Antiquarian & Secondhand Books

CCA BOOKSTORE
350 Sauchiehall Street
Glasgow G2 3JD
Tel:0141-353-1223 Art, Fiction, Poetry, Music & Film etc.

COOPER HAY RARE BOOKS
203 Bath Street
Glasgow G2 4HZ
Tel:0141-226-3074 Antiquarian Books, Maps & Prints

DILLONS THE BOOKSTORE
174/176 Argyle Street
Glasgow G2 8AH
Tel:0141-248-4814 Academic & General Books

DOWANSIDE BOOKS
Downside Lane
Glasgow G12 9B2
Tel:0141-334-3245 Antiquarian & Secondhand Books

FORBIDDEN PLANET
168 Buchanan Street
Glasgow G1 2LW
Tel:0141-331-1215 Science-fiction, Horror & Fantasy

FUTURESHOCK
89 Byres Road
Glasgow G11 5HN
Tel:0141-339-8184 Science-fiction Books

ROBERT GIBSON & SONS LTD
17 Fitzroy Place
Glasgow G3 7SF
Tel:0141-248-5674 Children's Books & Adult Fiction

GILMOREHILL BOOKS
43 Bank Street
Glasgow G12 6NE
Tel:0141-339-7504 Secondhand & Remainder Books

JORDANHILL COLLEGE BOOKSHOP
76 Southbrae Drive
Glasgow G13 1PP
Tel:0141-954-3533 Teachers' Education Books

KELVIN BOOKS LTD
Unit 19, Chapel St Estate
Maryhill
Glasgow G20 9BD
Tel:0141-945-5006 Educational & Academic Texts

JOHN MENZIES LTD
36 Argyle Street
Glasgow G2 8AP
Tel:0141-204-0636 General Books

JOHN MENZIES LTD
177 Sauchiehall St. Centre
Glasgow
Tel:0141-331-2833 General Books

JOHN MENZIES LTD
9 The Triangle
Bishopbriggs
Glasgow
Tel:0141-772-1160 General Books

MILNGAVIE BOOKSHOP
37 Douglas St
Milngavie
G62 6PE
Tel:0141-956-4752 School Supplies

MUSIC AT THE ALBA
61 Otago Street
Glasgow Printed music & scores

PICKERING & INGLIS
26 Bothwell Street
Glasgow G2 6PA
Tel:0141-221-8913 Christian & Scottish Books

PRIVATE LINES
319 Gallowgate
Glasgow
Tel:0141-556-1206 General Books

RIAS BOOKSHOP★
545 Sauchiehall St
Glasgow G3 7PQ
Tel:0141-221-6496 Architecture & Design Books
★moving to Princes Square, Buchanan St

ST PAUL MULTIMEDIA
5a-7 Royal Exchange Square
Glasgow G1 3HA
Tel:0141-226-3391 Religious Books etc.

JOHN SMITH & SON
57-61 St Vincent St
Glasgow G2 5TB
Tel:0141-221-7472 General Books

JOHN SMITH & SON
252 Byres Road
Glasgow G12
Tel:0141-334-2769 General Books

JOHN SMITH & SON
Glasgow University Bookshop
John McIntyre Building
University Avenue
Glasgow G12 8PP
Tel:0141-339-1463/334-1210 Academic &
Medical Books

JOHN SMITH & SON
The Curran Building
100 Cathedral Street
Glasgow G4 0LN
Tel:0141-552-3377 Academic Books

TRONGATE BOOKS
Unit 25, Candleriggs Market
Bell Street
Glasgow G1 1NU
Tel:0141-552-1545 Antiquarian & Secondhand Books

VOLTAIRE & ROUSSEAU
18 Otago Lane
Glasgow G12
Tel:0141-339-1811 Antiquarian & Secondhand Books

WATERSTONE'S
45-50 Princes Square
Glasgow G1 3JN
Tel:0141-221-9650 General Books

WATERSTONE'S
132 Union Street
Glasgow G1 3QQ
Tel:0141-221-0890 General Books

WESLEY OWEN BOOKS & MUSIC
160 Buchanan Street
Glasgow G1 2LL
Tel:0141-332-9431 Christian Books

WORD OF MOUTH
c/o Moon
The Studio
519 Great Western Road
Glasgow
Tel:0141-357-4282 Food, Drink & Cookery Books

Further reading...

Simon Berry and Hamish Whyte, eds., *Glasgow Observed* (Edinburgh:John Donald, 1987).

Moira Burgess, *Glasgow Books and Writers of the Twentieth Century: novelists, poets and playwrights: a select bibliography* (Glasgow: Book Trust Scotland, 1990).

Moira Burgess, *The Glasgow Novel; a survey and bibliography* (Motherwell and Glasgow: Scottish Library Association and Glasgow District Libraries, 2nd ed. 1986).

Moira Burgess and Hamish Whyte, eds., *Streets of Stone: an anthology of Glasgow short stories* (Edinburgh: Salamander press, 1985; reissued Mainstream, 1989).

Moira Burgess and Hamish Whyte, eds., *Streets of Gold: contemporary Glasgow stories* (Edinburgh: Mainstream, 1989).

George Eyre-Todd, *The Glasgow Poets* (Paisley: Alexander Gardner, 1903).

James A. Kilpatrick, *Literary Landmarks of Glasgow* (Glasgow: Saint Mungo Press, 1989).

Hamish Whyte, ed., *Mungo's Tongues: Glasgow poems 1630-1990* (Edinburgh: Mainstream, 1993).

Sheila Livingstone and Don Martin, *Canal Poets Anthology* (Strathkelvin writing - forthcoming publication).

In Glasgow we all love culture.
Tae us it's like meat tae a vulture.
Literature, painting and sculpture,
the theatre, films and such
are grist tae our mill.
See Glasgow?
It's brill.

Frank Rodgers 1995

Frank Rodgers became a freelance writer and illustrator in 1987 having previously taught Art in Glasgow schools for seventeen years. His picture books are enormously successful and include popular and well-known titles such as *Can Piggles Do It?* (1991), *B is for Book!* (1992) and *The Pirate and the Pig* (1996). He also illustrates the popular *Mr Majeika* books. His first novel, *The Drowning Boy*, set in Glasgow in the 1950s, was published in 1992.

76